T0001806

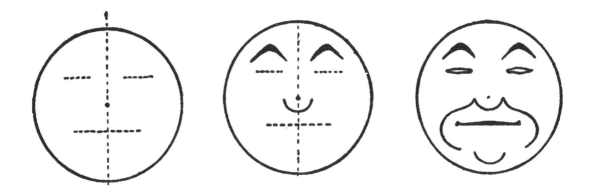

DRAWING MADE EASY

DRAWING MADE EASY

A HELPFUL BOOK FOR
YOUNG ARTISTS

THE WAY TO BEGIN AND FINISH YOUR SKETCHES
CLEARLY SHOWN STEP BY STEP

BY

E · G · LUTZ

APPLEWOOD BOOKS
Carlisle, Massachusetts

Copyright © 2024 Applewood Books, Inc.
An imprint of Arcadia publishing

Thank you for purchasing an Applewood book. Applewood
reprints America's lively classics—books from the past that
are still of interest to modern readers.

Our mission is to tell the authentic stories of people, places,
ideas, and history. In order to preserve the authenticity of the
works we publish, we do not alter the content in the editions
we reissue. Sometimes words, images, or ideas from the past
will seem inappropriate to the modern reader. We believe in
the value of presenting the past, just as it was, for the purposes
of informing the present and future.

978-1-4290-4654-1

MANUFACTURED IN THE UNITED STATES OF AMERICA
WITH AMERICAN-MADE MATERIALS

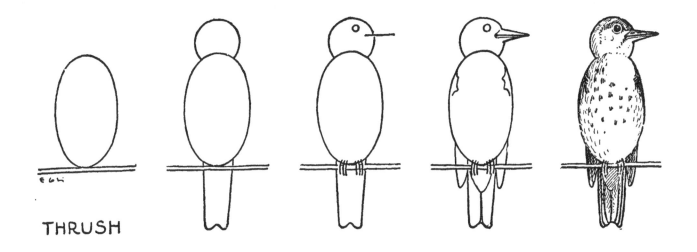

THRUSH

CONTENTS

CONTENTS

CONTENTS

PARRAKEETS

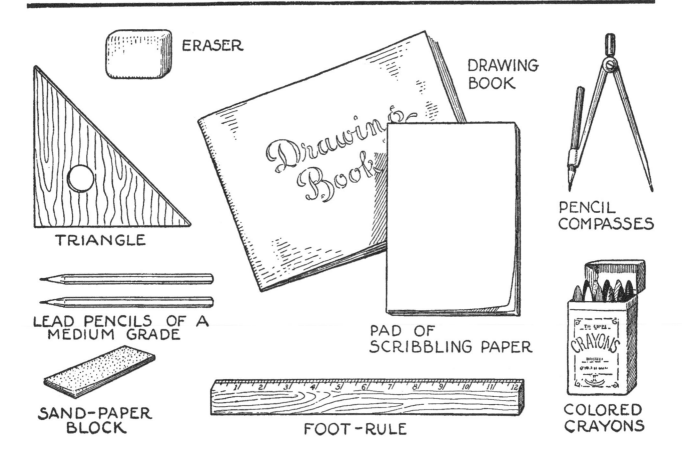

ERASER

DRAWING BOOK

TRIANGLE

PENCIL COMPASSES

LEAD PENCILS OF A MEDIUM GRADE

PAD OF SCRIBBLING PAPER

SAND-PAPER BLOCK

FOOT-RULE

COLORED CRAYONS

THINGS NEEDED FOR DRAWING

A lead-pencil and a pad of scribbling paper is about all you need in copying most of the pictures in this book. A soft rubber for erasing would be good to have, too. You might also get a small wooden triangle, a foot rule, and compasses with a pencil-point. These few tools are the modest representatives of the accurate instruments that inventors, engineers, and architects use in planning the things that we use every day. The house you live in, the vehicle in which you ride, and the machines that make the many things you wear and use were first planned and drawn out with the aid of dividers, compasses, rulers, and other drawing instruments.

Point the lead of your pencil on a block of sandpaper. No doubt you will want a water-color box. It is a good thing to have, but you can get lots of enjoyment in coloring your drawings with crayons.

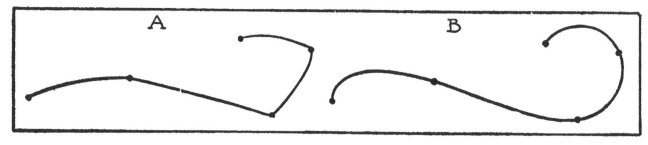

A. Not in this angular way—   **B.** But like this, in one continuous flowing curve.

DRAWING CURVES WITH THE HELP OF A SERIES OF DOTS

In the objects about us that we think of as beautiful, it isn't always their color that attracts or holds our attention. It is very often another matter; namely, their form or outline. For instance, in a vase, the gently curving lines of the form please as much as the color of the material. In flowers, leaves, and shells, the outlines that define the shapes delight the eye as well as the varied colors.

The diagrams on the opposite page are to suggest exercises in drawing that will help you to appreciate beauty in line as well as have you understand the importance of thinking while drawing. Make a series of scattered dots as shown. Be sure and have the dots at different distances apart. Now, if we take the first example, with the dots marked, 1, 2, 3, and 4: we start our line at the 1st dot, continue it to the 2d, and then to the 3d, and ending at the 4th. The idea is to make an easy flowing curved line from the first dot to the last. There must be no break or angular turning. In doing this, try to forget the pencil-point, and think only of a curved line that you are imagining as already marked on the paper going through the dots.

If you keep your eye on the pencil and watch it as you draw—the wrong way—the line will be like that in Diagram **A**, above, angular and wanting in beauty.

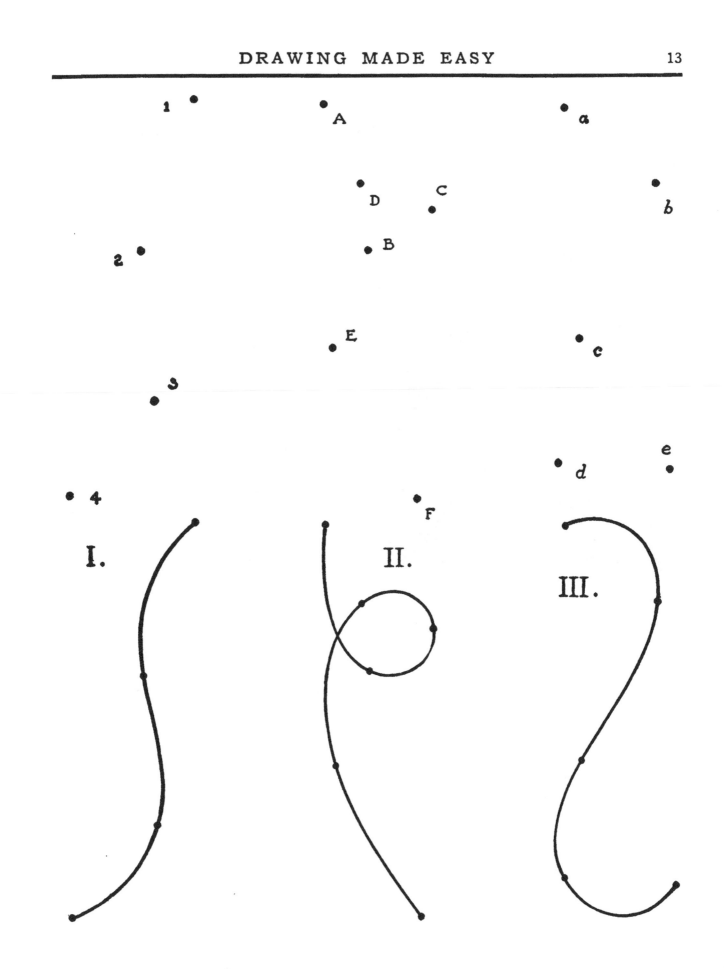

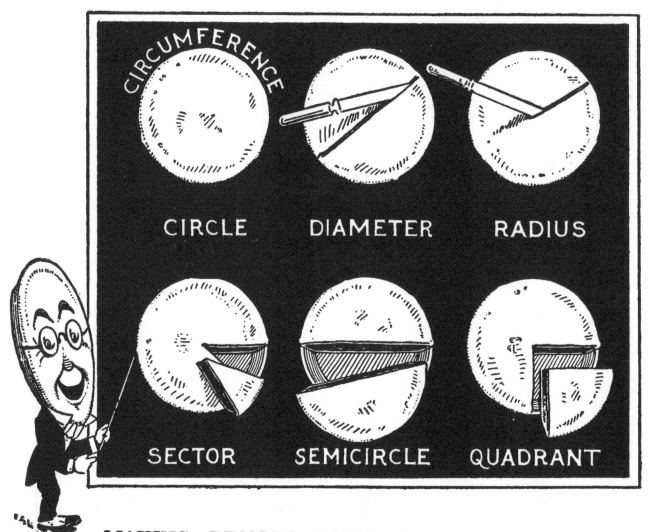

MAKING DESIGNS BASED ON A SQUARE AND WITH THE HELP OF THE COMPASSES

Some things about geometry are explained above in a way that no doubt will impress you. There will be no excuse, now, of not knowing the names of the different parts of a circle.

The first thing to do in making the designs on the other page is to construct a square. This can very easily be made with the foot rule and triangle. With the foot rule measure off the sides of the square of equal length, and with the triangle get the corners exactly right-angled.

The first seven designs are made by placing the point of the compasses in corners, as shown in B. In Figure 8 you have four other points to set your compasses, with which to draw more designs.

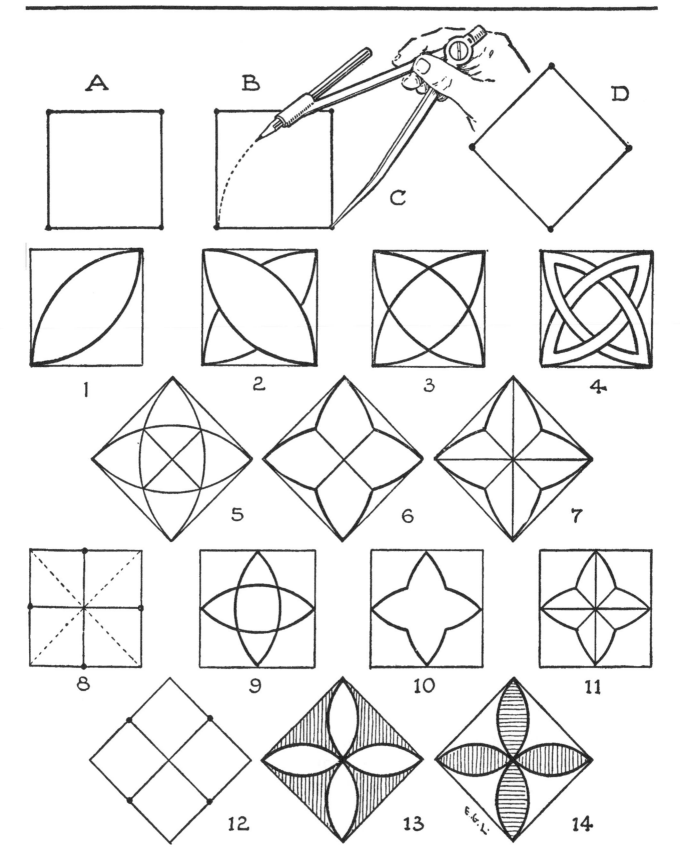

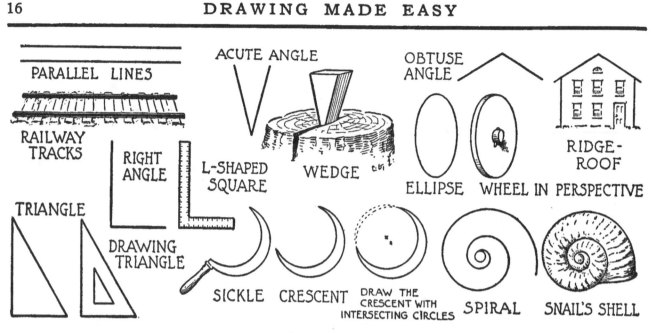

Similar forms in things and in geometrical figures.

DRAWING DESIGNS WITH THE COMPASSES AND WITH A CIRCLE AS A FOUNDATION

Draw a circle with the pencil compasses as shown in **A**, on the opposite page. Keep the legs of the compasses, when you have completed the circle, at the same distance apart as they were when describing it. Now this distance—the radius—if marked off around the circumference of the circle, will go exactly six times, as in **B**. (Turn back to page 14 again, to be reminded, by glancing at its picture, of the meaning of "radius" and "circumference.")

This dividing of a circle into six parts by marking the radius on its circumference is an unalterable law, and if you find that it does not come out this way, on your first attempt, it simply means that you must try again. When you have drawn a number of circles, and worked carefully in getting the points equally marked, you will have foundations for drawing the figures and designs on the remainder of the page. Figure 1, is a hexagon, or six-sided plane, while below it, Figure 4, is a triangle, or plane with three angles and three sides.

These designs, as well as those on page 15, made within a square, may be brightened up with the colored crayons.

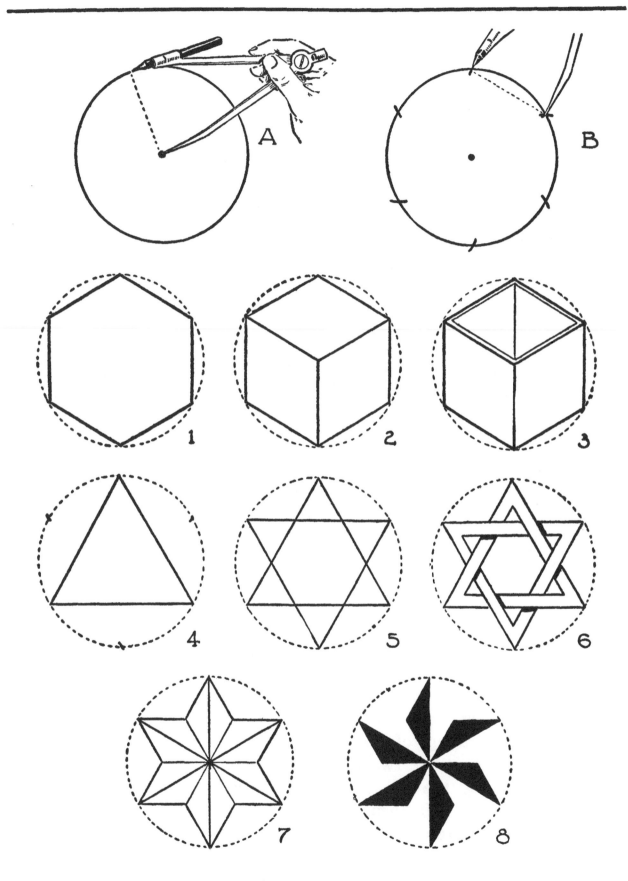

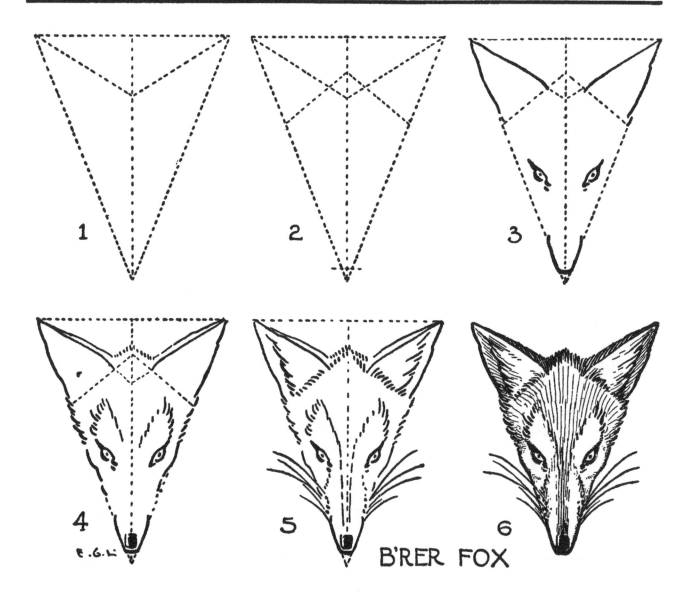

1

2

3

4

5   B'RER FOX

6

The first thing in drawing is to understand the form of that which we wish to picture. Some objects are so oddly formed and so full of detail that we must stop first and give a few minutes to study their form and the meaning of the detail. But there are other things of simpler form, and so easier to draw. The pictures on these two pages, for instance. It is very quickly grasped by the eye that their general outlines are bounded by triangles. If, then, a triangle is drawn first, as indicated in the first figure of each example, the rest of the drawing can be proceeded with very quickly.

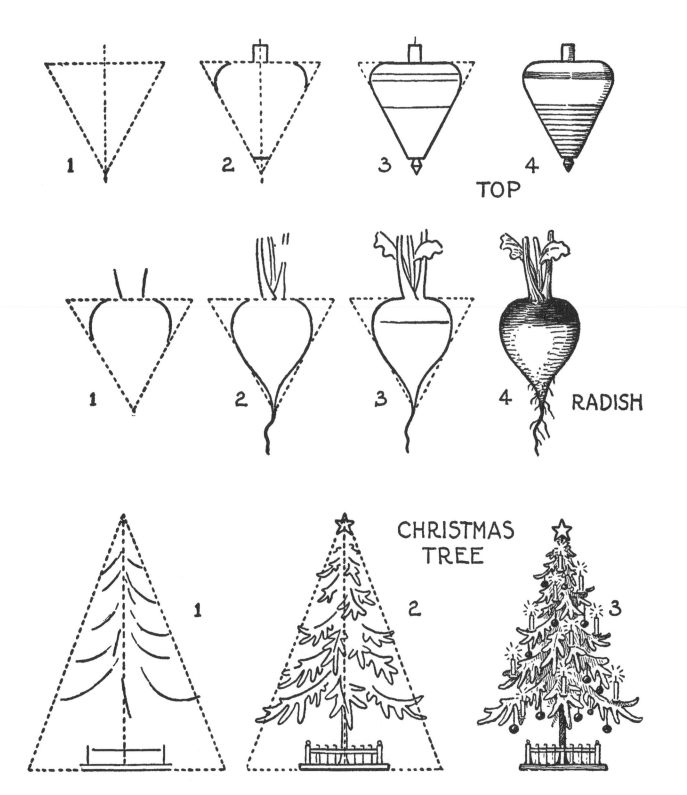

TOP

RADISH

CHRISTMAS
TREE

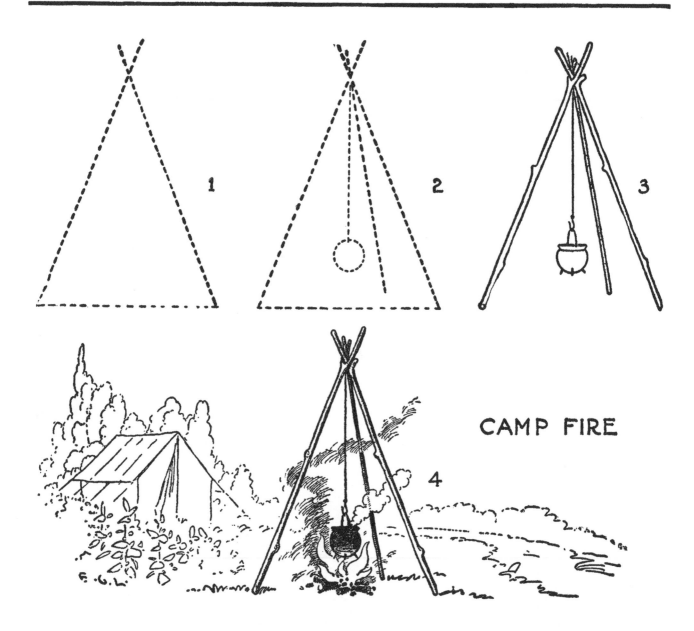

CAMP FIRE

Here are two more subjects that are very easy to draw if their characteristic forms—triangles—are first indicated.

It is not intended that the dotted lines in the diagrams are to be copied by you as dotted lines. Dotted lines in these examples, and in the diagrams throughout the book, merely represent construction lines that are to be marked faintly.

In going on with your drawing by following the lesson as indicated above, it is well to keep constantly in mind that it is the completed sketch, as in Figure 4, that you are endeavoring to copy.

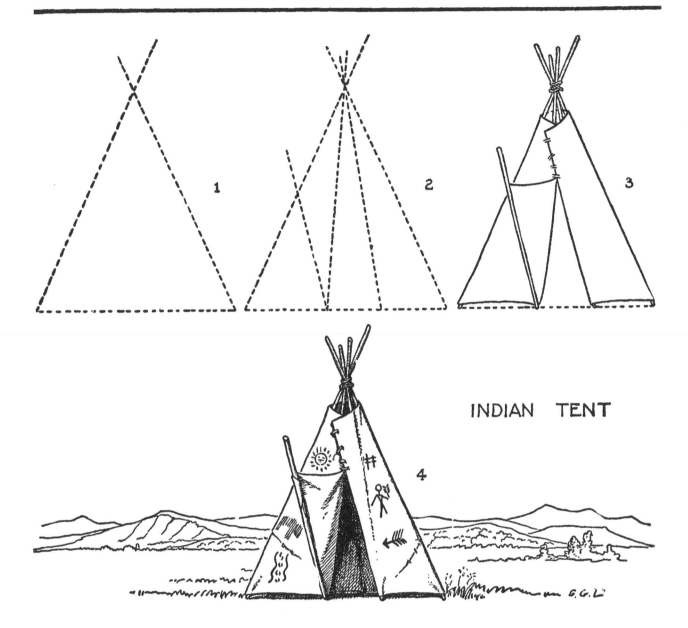

INDIAN TENT

It is very quickly understood, at the first glance, that the Red
   Indian's tent has a triangular outline.
The construction lines, which you have marked faintly, as suggested on the preceding page, need not be erased in completing
   the sketch. When you have copied the landscape, place in
   the distance a horse, or a buffalo. Farther on in the book
   are pages with pictures showing you how to proceed in picturing such subjects. You noticed, of course, while you were
   drawing this picture, that the flap of the tent and the open-
   ing are both triangular.

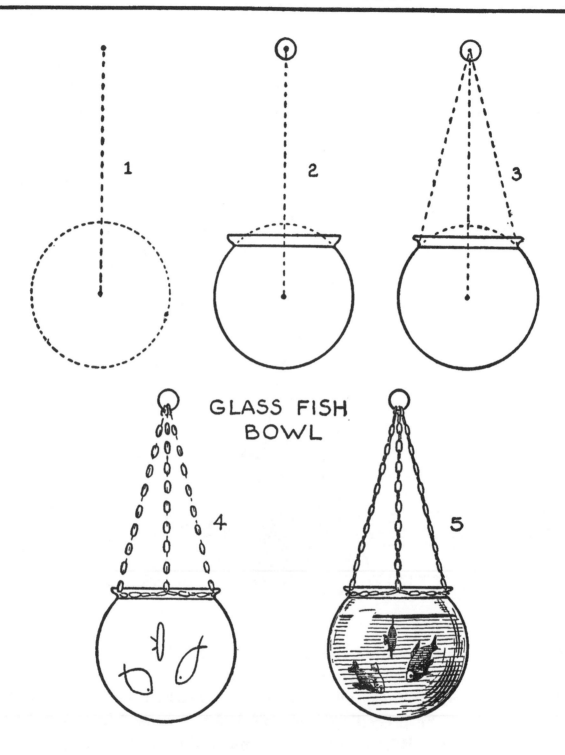

GLASS FISH
BOWL

Circles are made first in starting the subjects on these pages. Where the form is clearly a circle, the fish bowl above, for instance, use the compasses. But in picturing the cherries, the toy dog, or the radish, draw the circles free-hand.

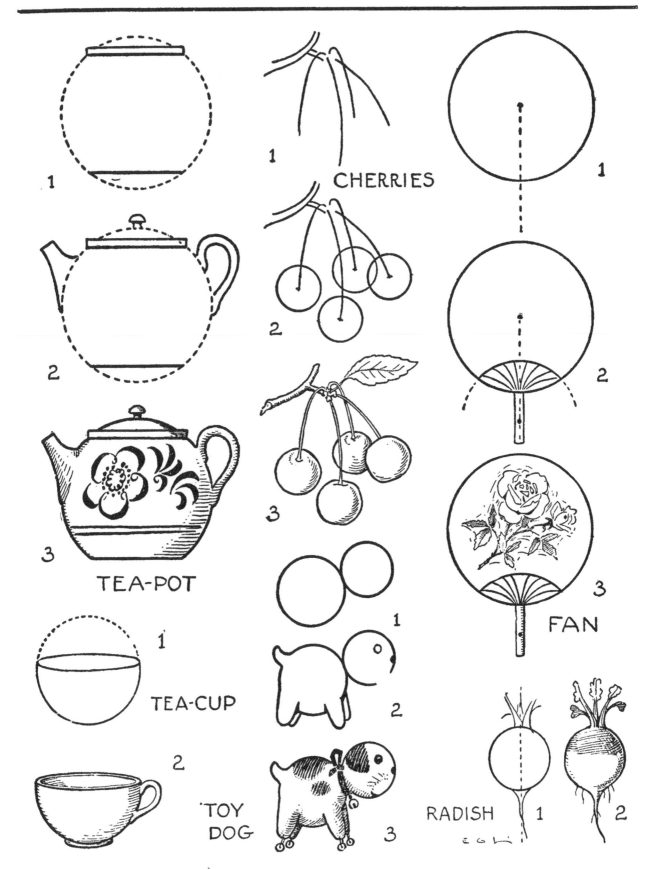

1

2

3

TEA-POT

1

TEA-CUP

2

CHERRIES

1

2

3

1

2

3

TOY
DOG

1

2

3

FAN

RADISH 1 2

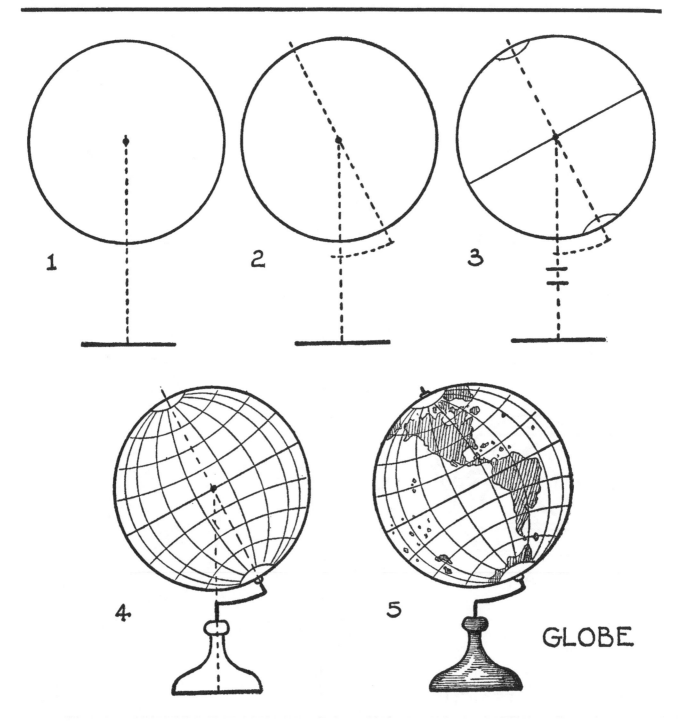

GLOBE

The terrestrial globe pictured on this page requires some very careful work with the compasses. For the middle line of the equator and the central line of the support use the ruler. In a subject such as this, where the lines are unmistakably straight, use a ruler.

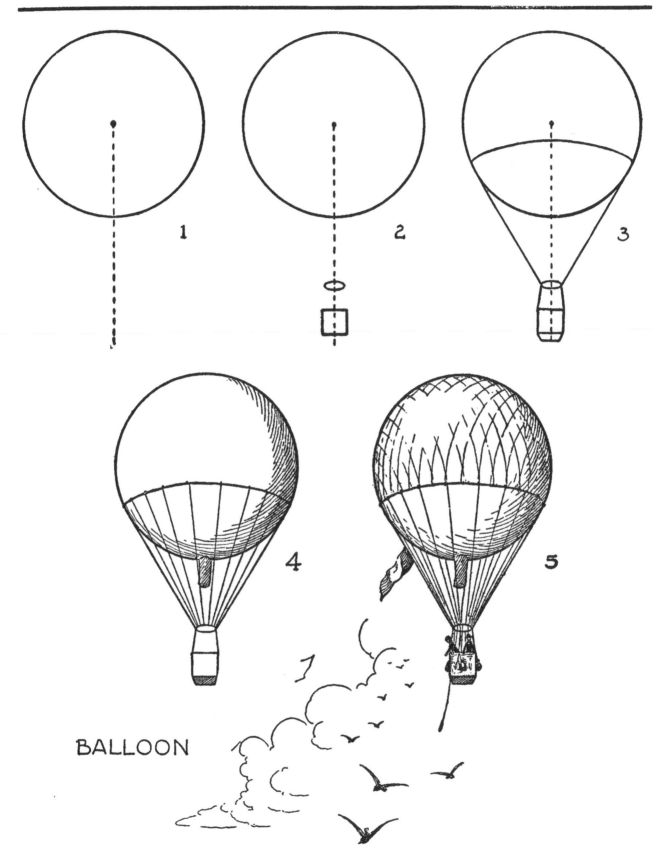

1

2

3

4

5

BALLOON

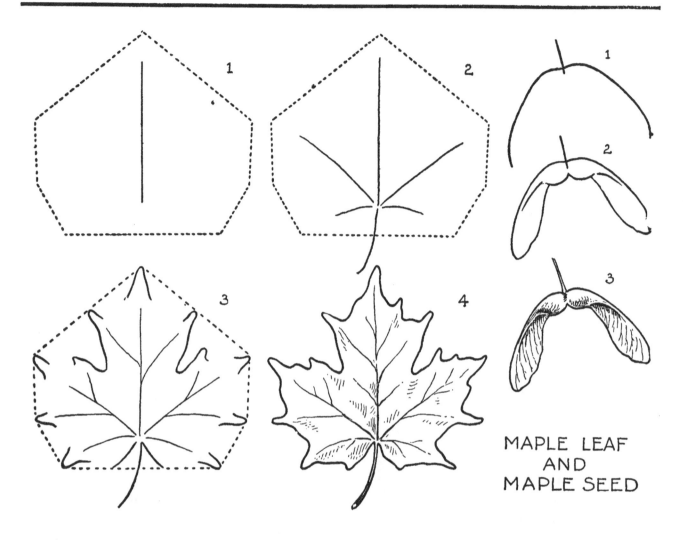

MAPLE LEAF
AND
MAPLE SEED

DRAWING LEAVES

During the summer you will find many leaves that can serve as patterns for drawing. The oak and the maple leaf are given here as examples.

If you try, in your first lines in copying one of these leaves, to mark the way the outline goes in and out, you will not get along very well. The best plan is to block out the entire space that the leaf takes up, and then draw the ribs, and after that the outline.

Be sure and draw other leaf-forms, those that you find in the woods, or on plants. Before you begin to sketch them, give some attention to their general form and mark that first. The little details are then much easier to put in their proper places.

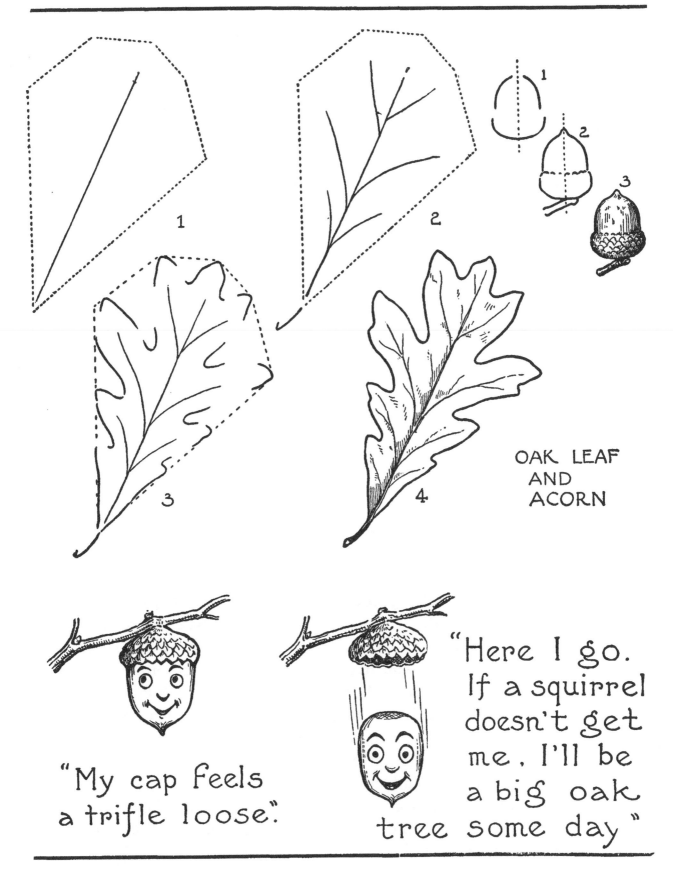

OAK LEAF
AND
ACORN

"My cap feels
a trifle loose".

"Here I go.
If a squirrel
doesn't get
me, I'll be
a big oak
tree some day"

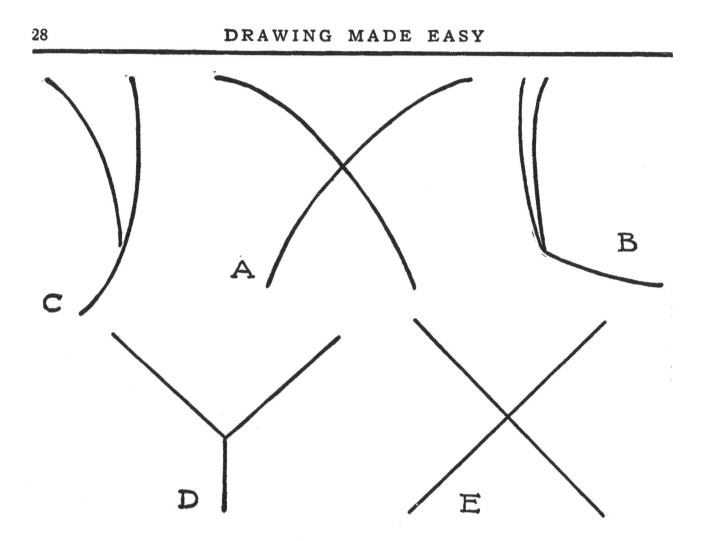

BUTTERFLIES

Making pictures of butterflies is not difficult. You will see on
pages 29 and 30 the progressive steps by which five different
kinds are pictured. In each case it is the last figure of each
series of diagrams that you are striving to copy. And Figure 1,
in each case, shows the first lines that you put on the paper.

It is also possible to draw butterflies in the way suggested for
drawing leaves; that is, marking out at the beginning the
whole space that the subject takes up.

But the five simple combinations of lines, grouped above, are so
expressive of our subjects, that marking them first makes a
very good way to start picturing the five butterflies.

Notice how one of these butterflies, in its construction lines, resem-
bles the letter Y, while two others suggest the letter X.

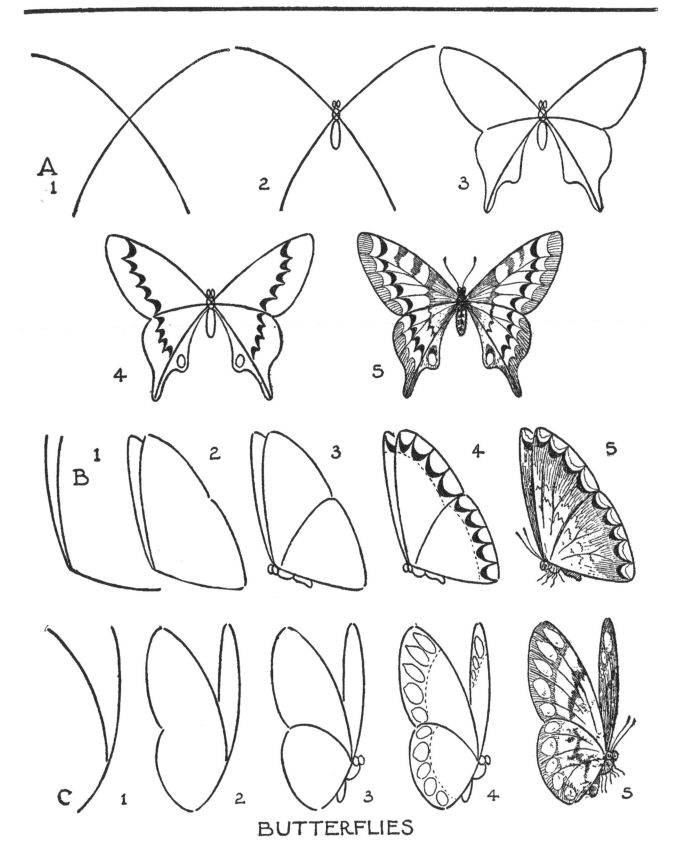

BUTTERFLIES

BUTTERFLIES

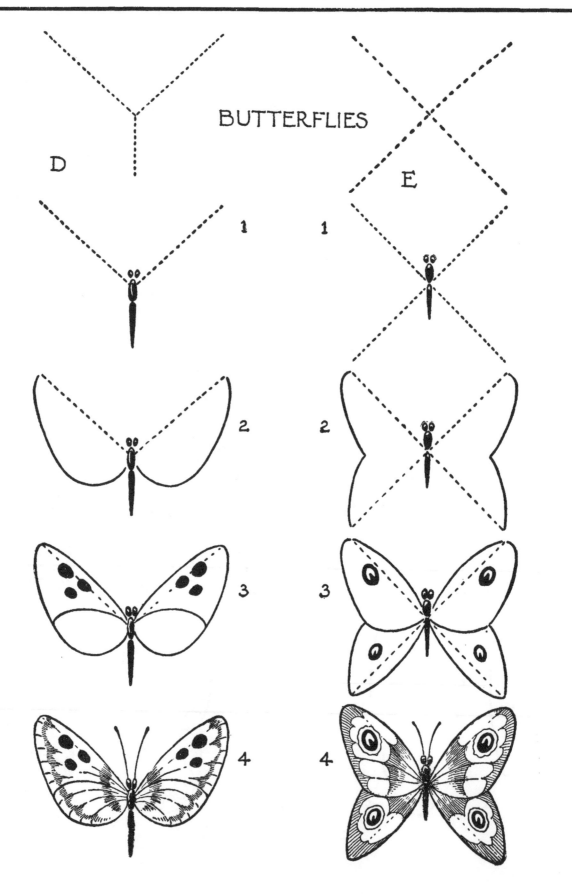

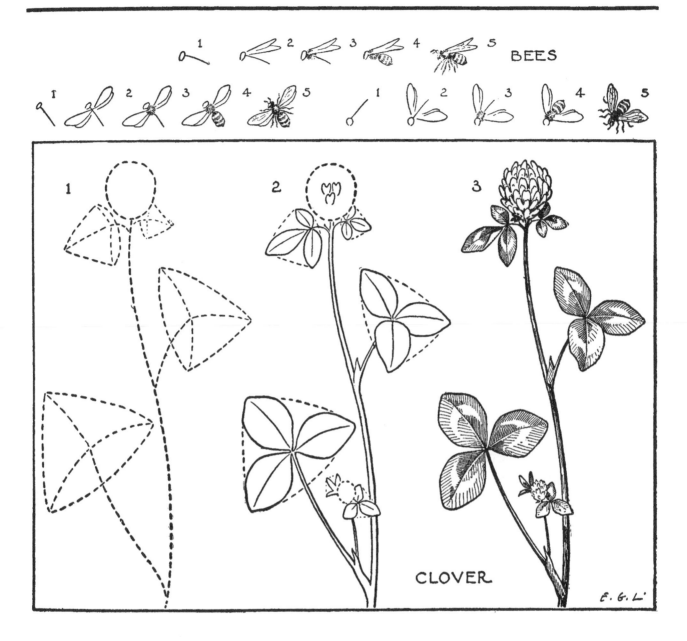

CLOVER

The series of diagrams on the top of this page show how to go
about making pictures of bees.

The clover blossom and leaves are blocked out first in lightly
marked lines, as indicated in Figure 1. Continue with the
work, and when you have finished it, as shown in Figure 3,
you may sketch a bee resting lightly on top of the clover blossom. That is the way you often see bees when they are gath-
ering honey in the summertime. And remember to indicate
one flying to the hive with his gathered honey and pollen.

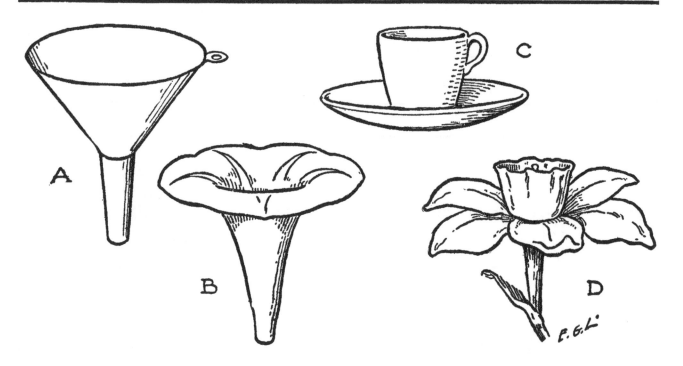

The engraving above shows us the resemblance between a morning-glory and a funnel, and the likeness of a narcissus to a cup and saucer.

Now, the idea of showing these comparisons is to help you understand the forms of these flowers. As you know, it is a great help in drawing to understand thoroughly the form of the particular object that we are drawing. Take the morning-glory, for instance; by keeping in mind its striking resemblance to a funnel, a very simple thing to picture, we are able to visualize it in simple lines and so sketch it easily.

And in the narcissus; if you do not allow the minor divisions to bother you, but see at once the resemblance to a cup and saucer, you will know how to go about the work of drawing with much more facility. That is, you will plan as your start some form like a cup and its saucer, as shown in Figure 2 of the narcissus diagrams on the opposite page.

The pictures of bees and butterflies that you now know how to make will be good to combine with the flower sketches that you will learn to draw from the lessons on the five following pages.

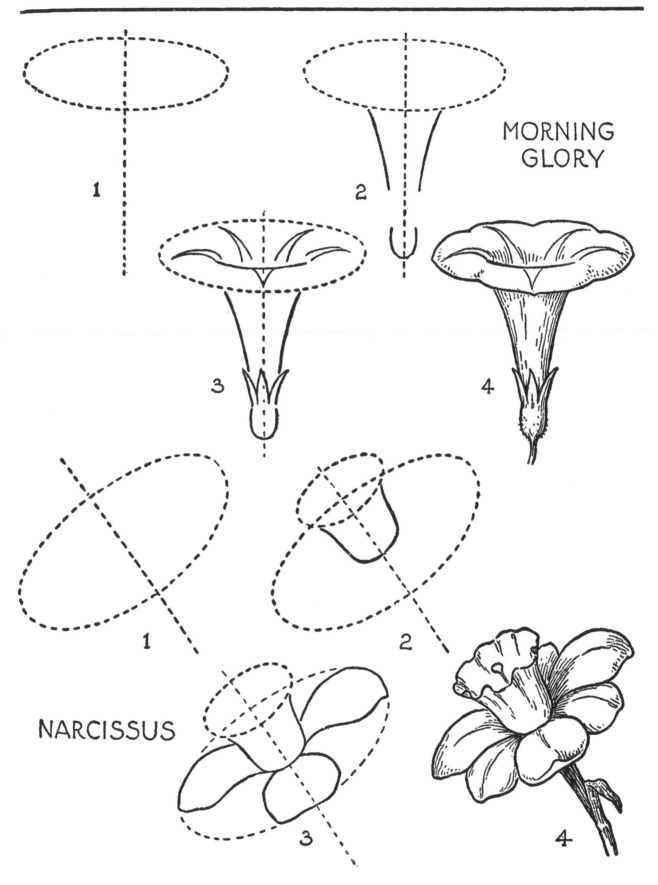

MORNING
GLORY

1

2

3

4

NARCISSUS

1

2

3

4

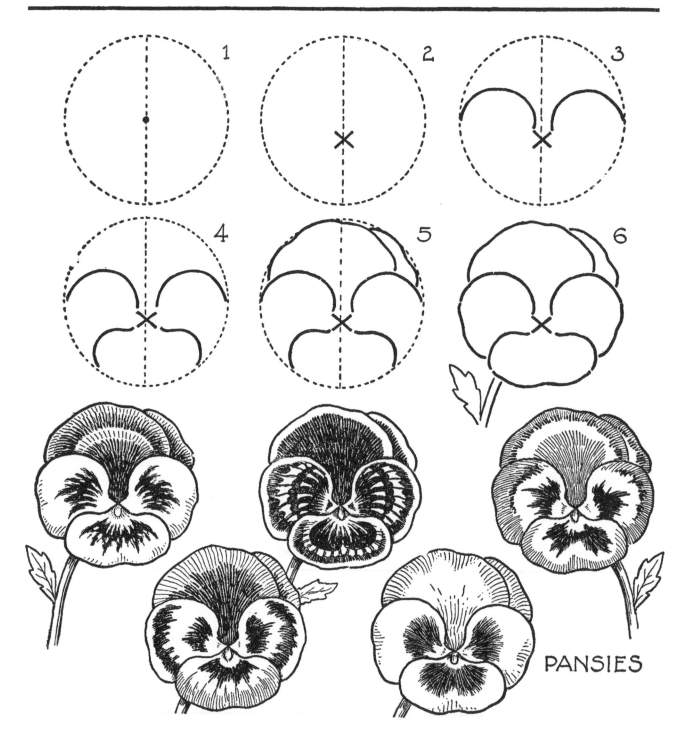

PANSIES

The six diagrams above show how to draw the outlines of a pansy, and the five varied-patterned pansies below give a hint for finishing with the pencil or crayons.

The picturing of buttercups and daisies is explained on the opposite page.

BUTTERCUPS
AND DAISIES

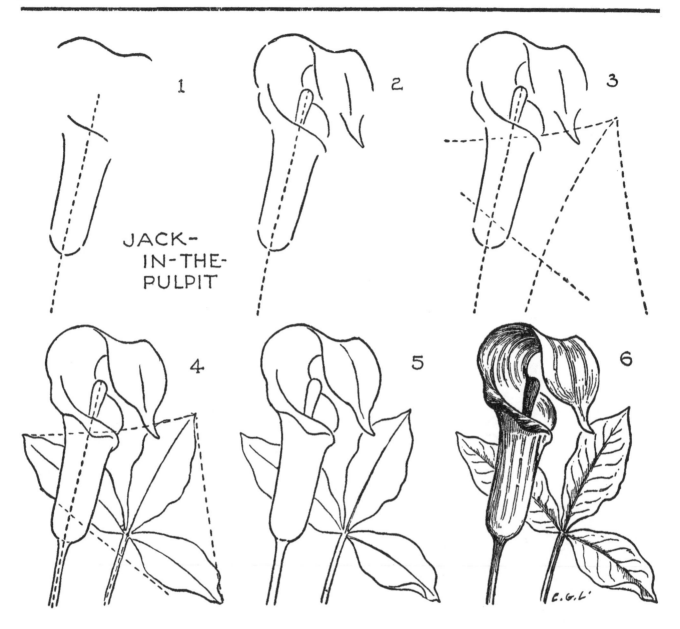

JACK-
IN-THE-
PULPIT

In beginning to draw the Jack-in-the-pulpit pictured above, the important line for you to consider is the one representing the centre of the flower, or its axis. Marking this lightly, and always keeping it in mind as you draw, helps to place properly other parts or details of the subject.

This flower, which you may find early in the spring, growing in moist places in the woods, is a cousin to the large white calla-lily of the conservatory.

Sketching the fuchsia is also made easier by noting the central imagined lines that go through the open flower and the bud.

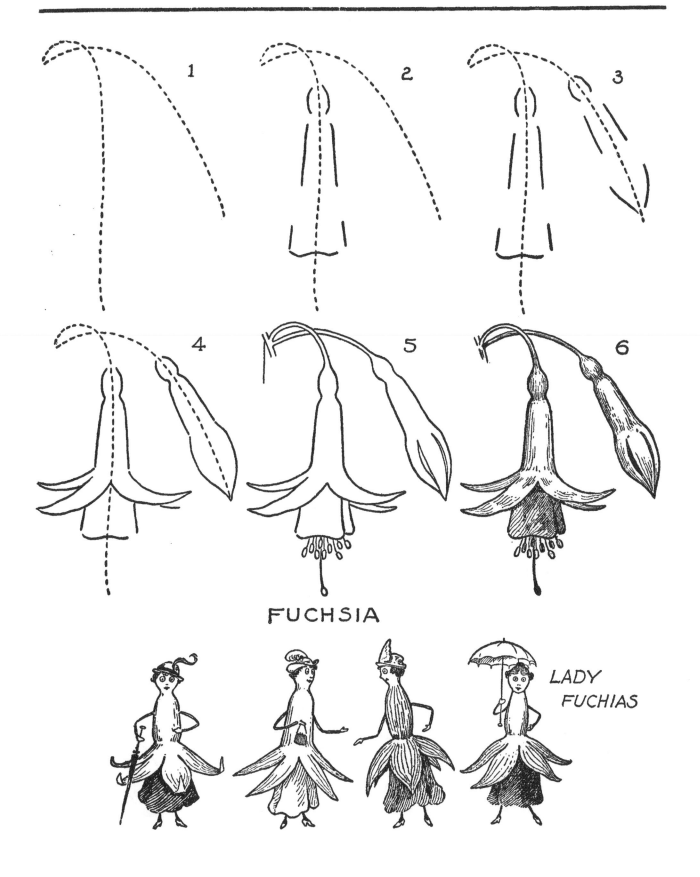

FUCHSIA

LADY
FUCHIAS

RABBITS

Here are four rabbits that will very patiently pose for you while you sketch them.

It doesn't matter which one of them you begin on, as the mode of procedure in each case is the same in marking an elliptical, or oval form, as the first stroke of your pencil.

In drawing one of these rabbits, keep your eye and mind most of the time on his picture, as shown above, but glance from time to time at the series of diagrams to see the progressive manner that you follow to complete his picture.

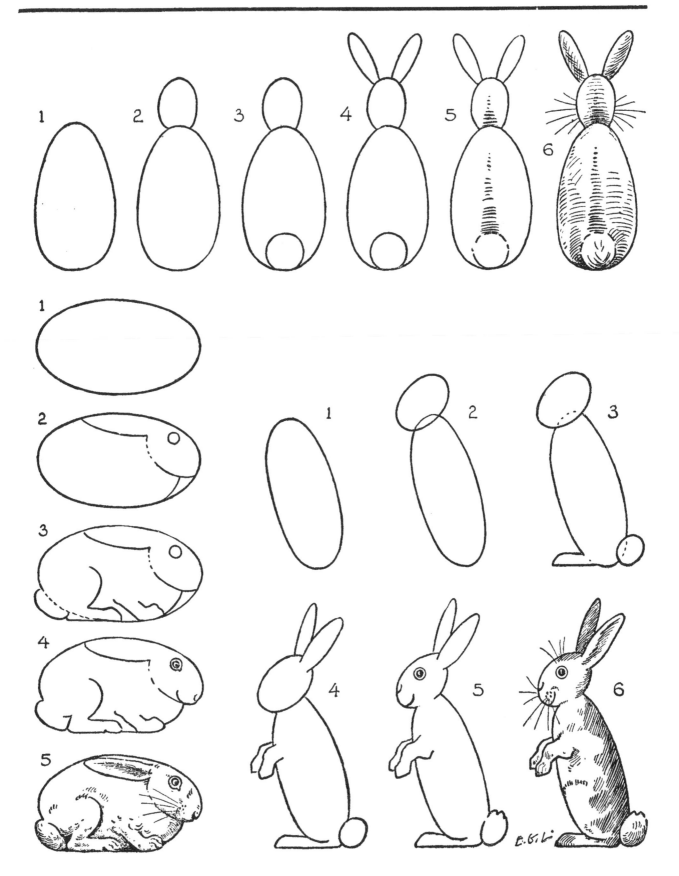

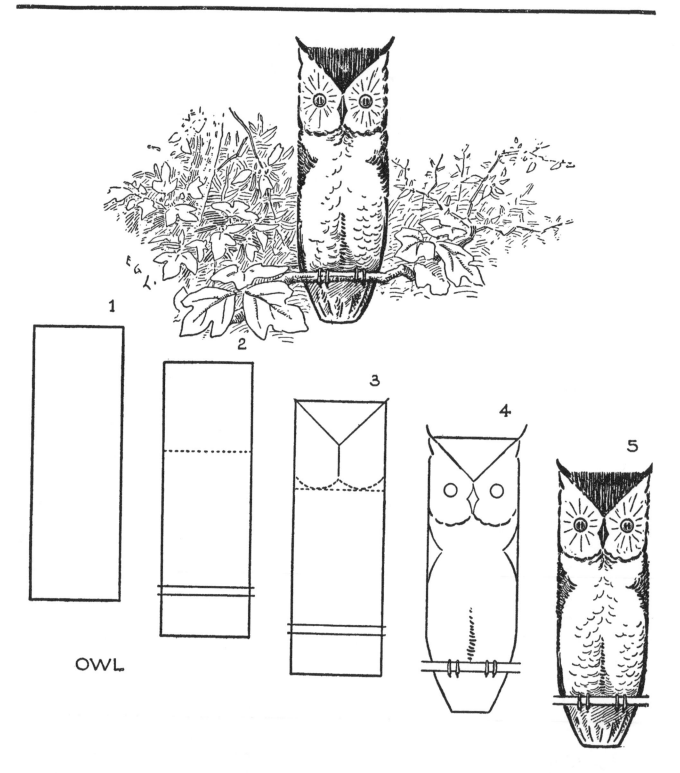

1

2

3

4

5

OWL.

Owls are very obliging and friendly models. When you go to the
Zoo do not fail to try your hand at sketching them. It will
not be at all difficult, for your owl model will most likely keep
very still and only blink his eyes.

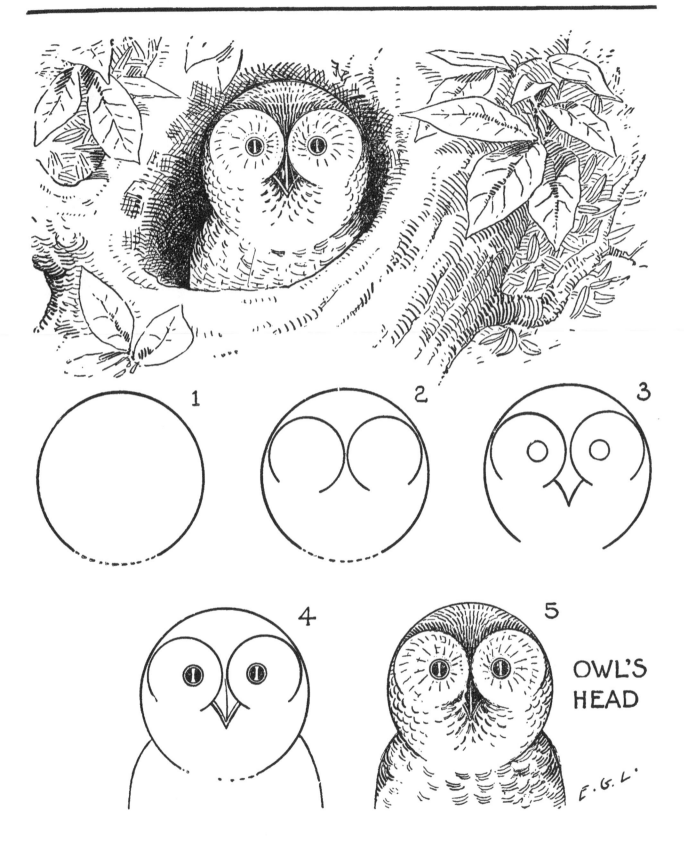

OWL'S
HEAD

Mark the first lines faintly and get them as round as possible,
entirely by free hand.

DUCK AND PENGUIN

Other birds at the Zoo that sometimes keep quiet long enough for you to sketch are the ducks, geese, and cranes. Often they rest themselves on one leg and stay that way for some time. Drawing a bird in this position is not so easy as it seems. Picturing him balanced on one leg, and not as if he were toppling over, is a matter of careful consideration of what pencil strokes to put down at the start.

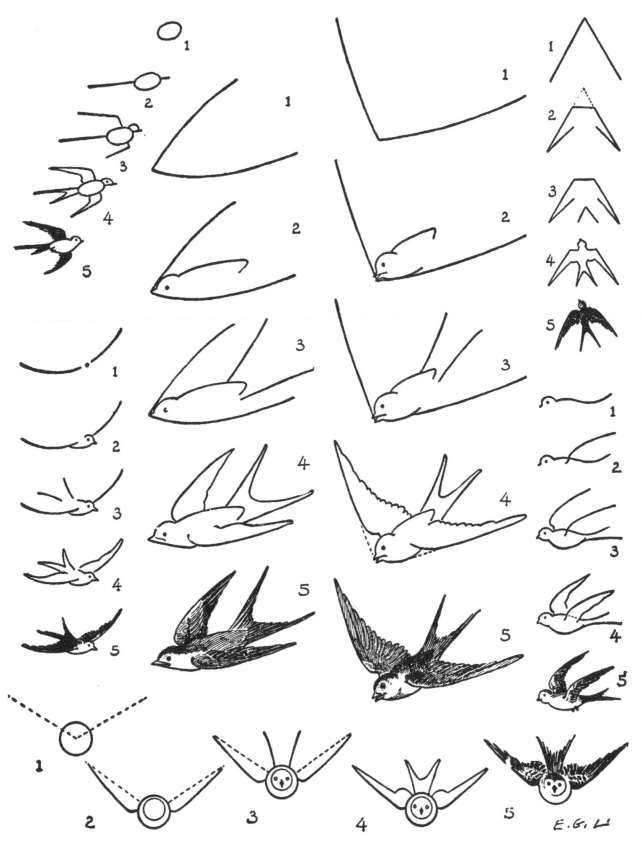

Swallows.

1

2

3

GOOSE   4

5

6

DUCK   1

2

3

4

5

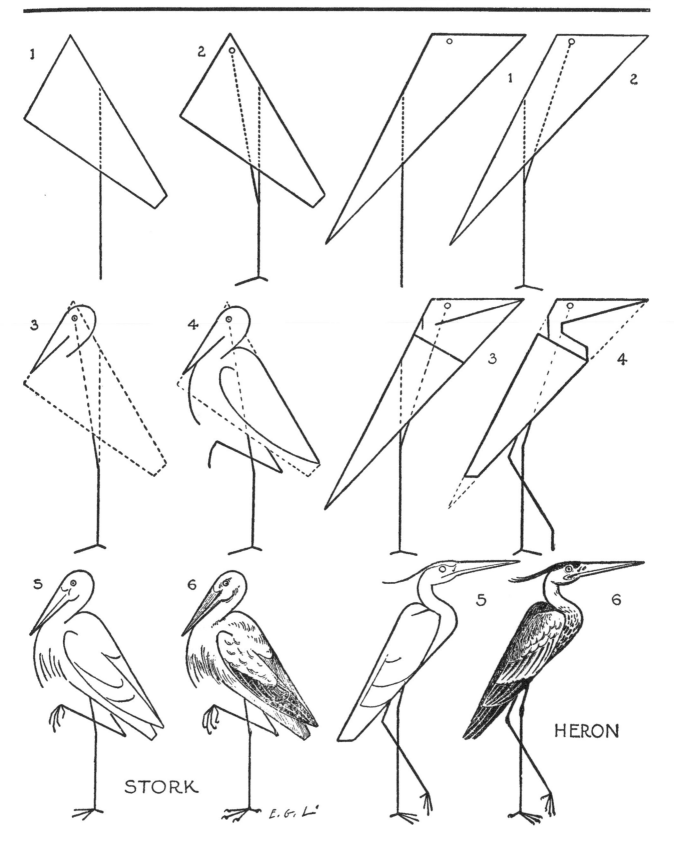

STORK

E. G. L.

HERON

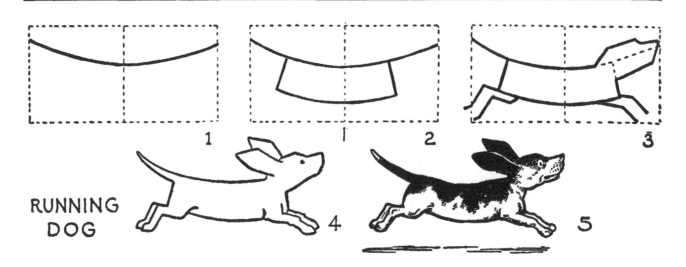

RUNNING
DOG

The kind of elephant that one commonly sees at the Zoo is the Indian elephant. He has a thick-set body and small ears. Sometimes, however, we see the African elephant. You will know one of this kind at once by his huge ears. The ears look, especially when the elephant moves them, like large fans. There are other unlikenesses between these two elephants, but this difference in the size of the ear is the principal one.

There are shown on the opposite page the progressive steps in making pictures of these two elephants.

To draw the running dog pictured above, first construct two squares side by side, indicated by dotted lines, and then mark a firm curved line, as in Figure 1. When you have proceeded as far as the next step, drawing the body, you will have some resemblance to the complete sketch shown by Figure 5. An odd way is given below of drawing the droll face of a monkey by making a circle and then a smaller one intersecting it below.

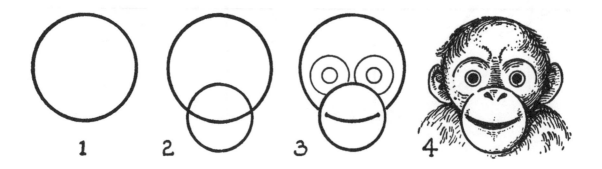

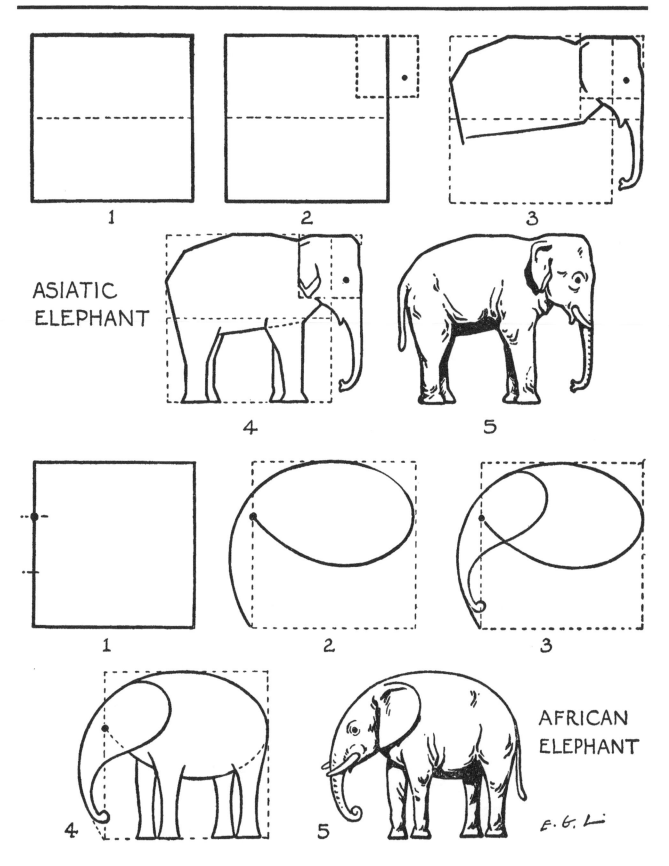

ASIATIC
ELEPHANT

AFRICAN
ELEPHANT

DRAWING A PIG WITH A SINGLE LINE
AND WITH THE EYES CLOSED

Here we have the picture of a pig in a simple outline. It is a copy for you to follow. But you are to make your drawing in a peculiar manner; that is, with the eyes closed, or not looking at the paper, and in one unbroken line. Now, drawing in this way, by which the inner vision only is used, the attention is called to one great fact about drawing. It is this:

Drawing is first a matter of the mind and then
only secondly a thing of pencil and paper.

When you are trying this little exercise of drawing a pig with the eyes closed and without lifting the pencil from the paper, so as to get one continuous line you are forced to hold and keep in your mind the picture of a pig. You can understand then that although we need pencil, brushes, and paints in picture making, the first thing needed is an idea or an image in the mind of that which we wish to portray.

On the opposite page are two types of pigs; the one is of a somewhat square character in his outline, while the other is a jolly round fat one.

Diagrams 2 and 3, of the pig of a square character, are good examples of the blocking-out method in drawing.

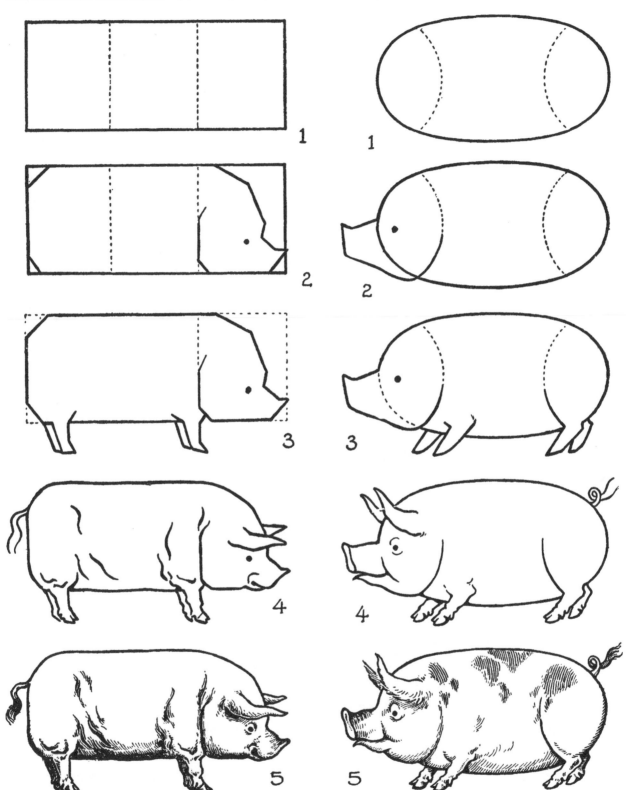

Pigs.

CAT AND MICE

In drawing the very much surprised cat with the bold black mouse in front of her—the picture on the opposite page—a vertical, or up-and-down line, going through the centres of the two forms with which the drawing is started helps to keep these animals in their correct positions.

It is plain to be seen that the right way of beginning to draw a mouse is to make a simple form that gives a general idea of his body, as the mere addition of a curlicue for a tail at once gives a fairly good portrait of a mouse.

If the cat on this page were to turn around, all the mice would scamper away. That is a good way to draw them. Try it.

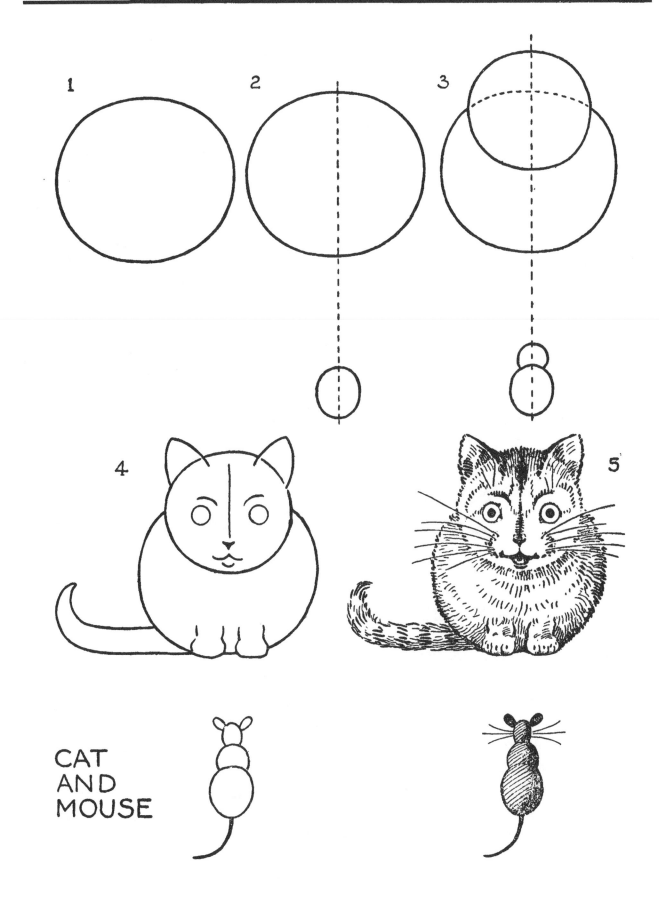

1

2

3

4

5

CAT
AND
MOUSE

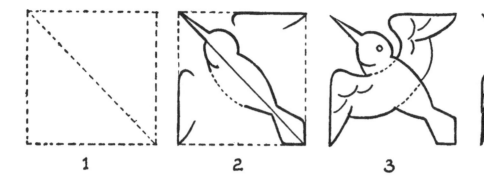

BIRD, SNAIL, TORTOISE, AND FISH

After school-days comes vacation time, when you will spend many happy hours in the woods and fields. But do not with all your outdoor play neglect drawing. Good subjects to sketch will most likely come your way. A tortoise, that during a ramble may cross your path, will make an easy subject to draw. The shell suggests an inverted cup.

The flicker, as you will notice, has two toes in front and two pointing backward. Notice how he uses his tail feathers to support himself as he taps the tree trunk.

SQUIRREL

CHIPMUNK

FLICKER

THRUSH

E.G.L.

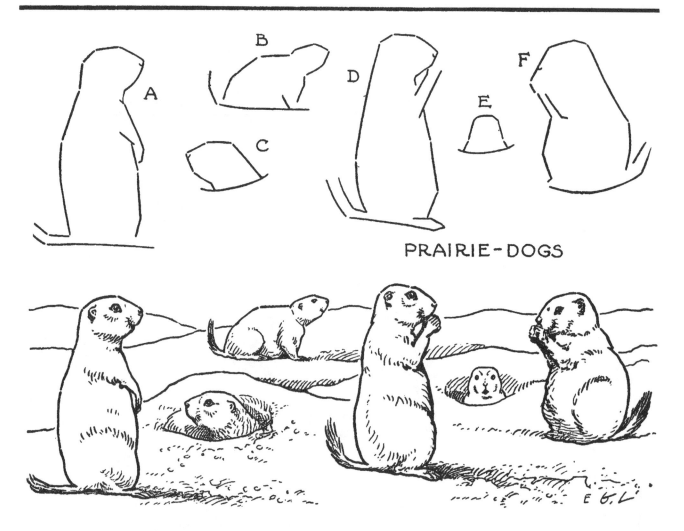

PRAIRIE-DOGS

You can learn to draw a buffalo in a standing position by following the series of diagrams on the page opposite. The crinkly mass of the buffalo's head is rather hard to represent in lines with a lead-pencil. The proper tool would be a brush filled with color with which you could paint quickly the large mass of hair and get the outline soft and woolly, as it really is in nature. However, you will learn something by trying to do the best you can in following the lesson on the page. Afterward you may paint his picture with a brush and color.

The prairie-dogs really haven't very strongly defined character. Some character they have, of course, but it is merely that they are fat little bodies. The simple outlines at the top show what you are to draw first to indicate this character.

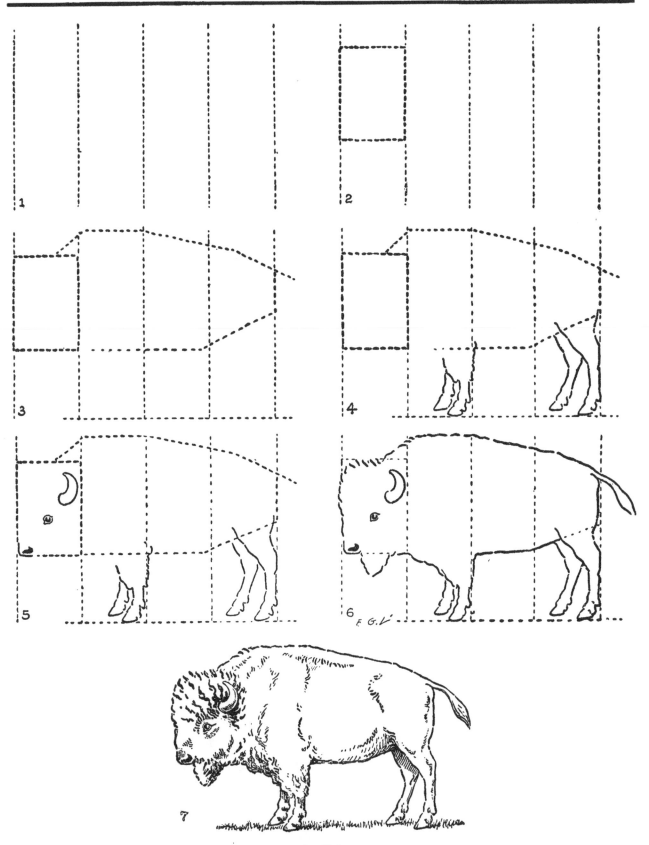

Buffalo.

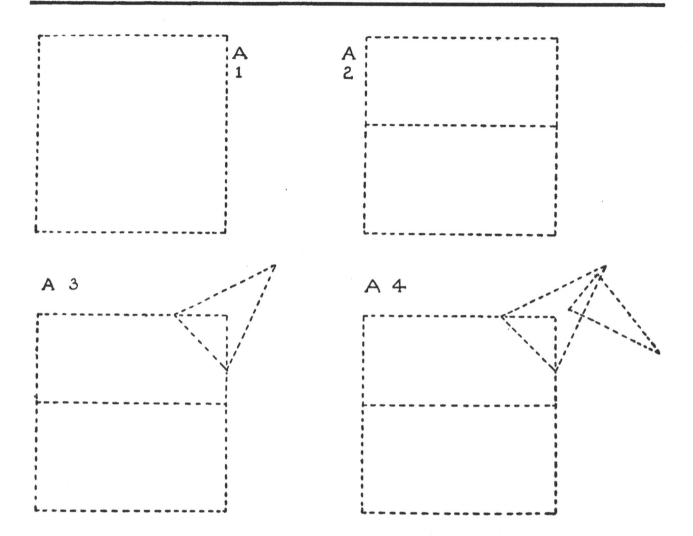

The engravings on this and the three following pages show you how
   to make pictures of horses.

In the first lesson, you start your sketch with a square. Draw it
   free-hand; that is, without the aid of ruler or triangle. Make
   it as accurately as possible and then divide it into two parts
   by a line across it just above the middle. Now, in one corner
   mark a triangle pointing obliquely upward and another triangle slanting downward. The exact procedure is shown
   above. All the lines that you have been marking so far should
   be made faintly, as they are only construction lines. The
   lesson is continued in the five diagrams on the next page.

The other horses, series B, C, D, and E, on the following pages, are
   to be drawn step by step, as shown in the diagrams.

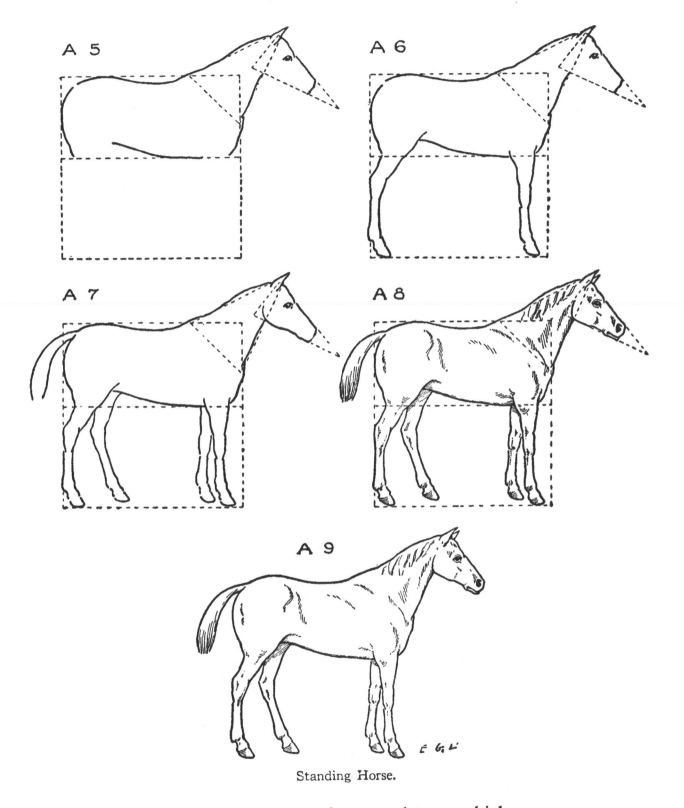

Standing Horse.

Draw this horse as he appears harnessed to a vehicle.

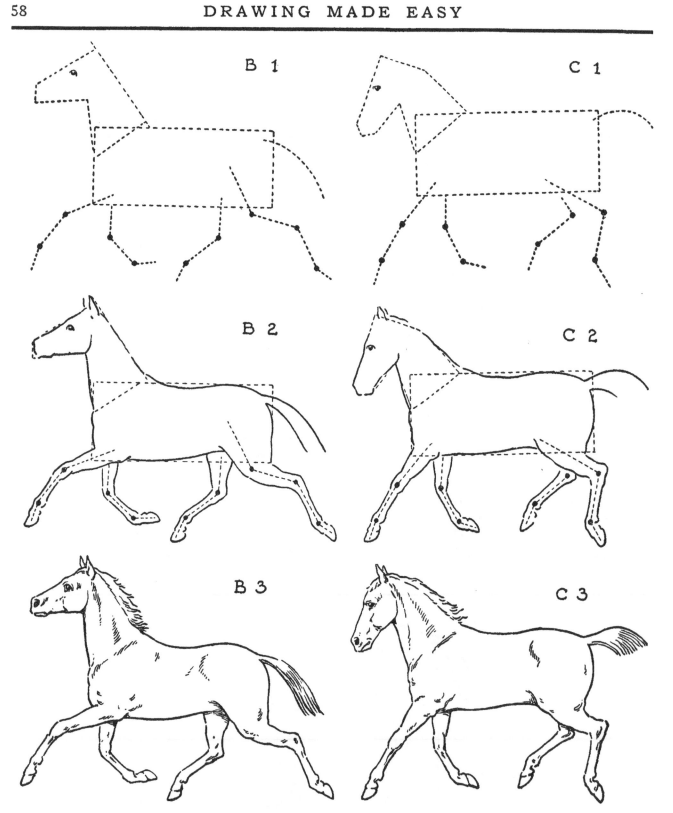

Horses in Movement.

While drawing these horses, keep the general proportions in mind, as illustrated by the four diagrams on page 56.

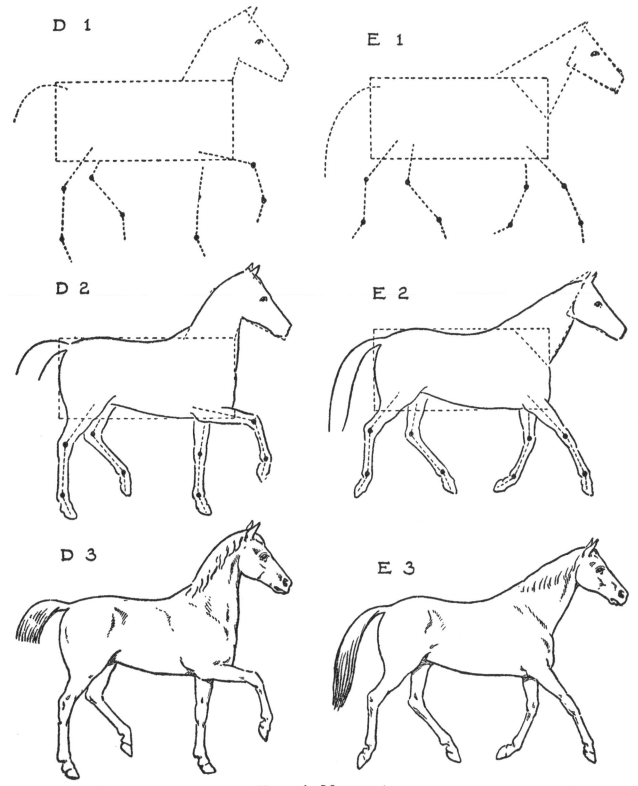

D 1   E 1

D 2   E 2

D 3   E 3

Horses in Movement.

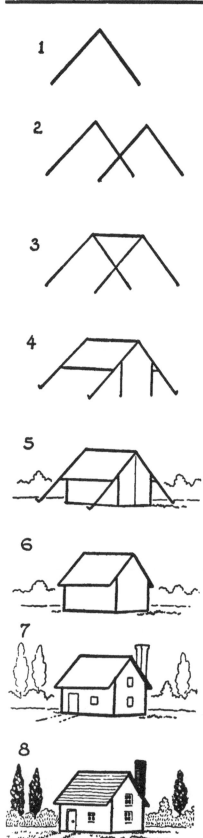

On this page are two lessons in drawing houses that have a little of the whimsical about the way that we go about in picturing them.

In one case a start is made by marking a V turned upside down. The picture soon becomes a tent and then a house when a chimney is added. In the other case a house is built pictorially by progressive steps that begin by the drawing of a lozenge-shaped design.

There is no need to hesitate when about to sketch the sailboat illustrated on the opposite page. A triangle, quickly drawn, gives the idea of a sail at once, and with the addition of a line for the mast and an indication of the hull, we have the picture almost completed. The tugboat is made by sketching, with strict regard to their proportions, the hull and then the smoke-stack. These are the two most conspicuous parts, and so it is good to indicate them at once.

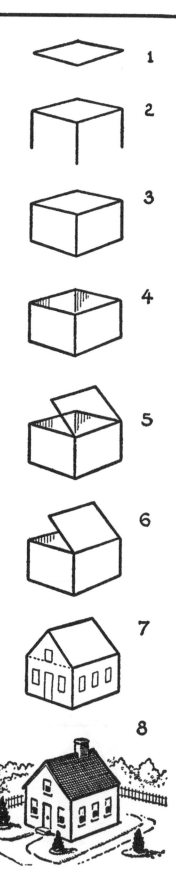

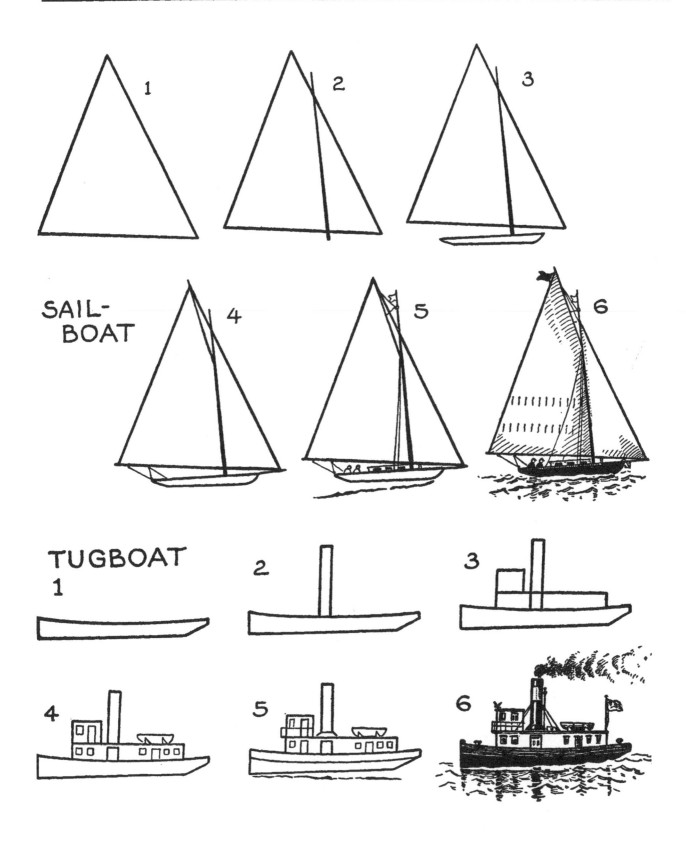

SAIL-
BOAT

TUGBOAT

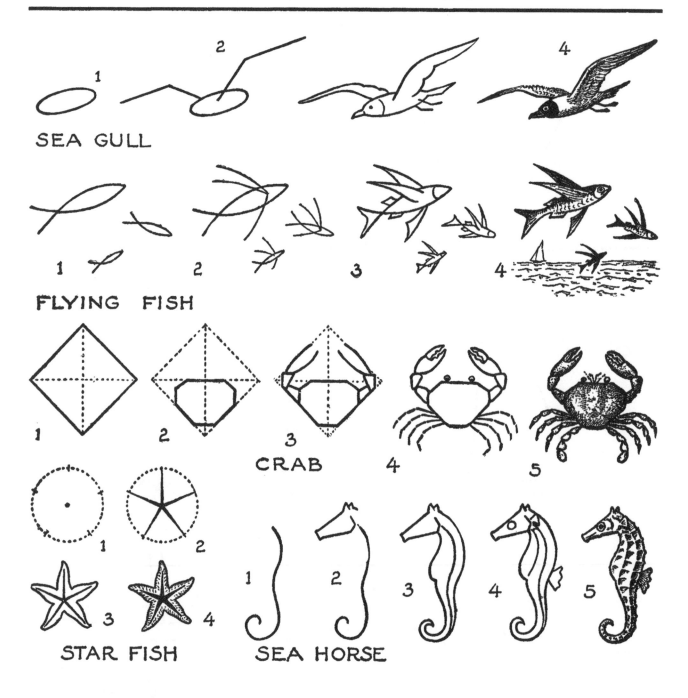

SEA GULL, FLYING FISH, CRAB, STAR FISH, SEA HORSE

A few forms of ocean life are portrayed here. If you have not been so fortunate as to have seen these creatures in life at the sea-shore, or in aquariums, you are at least familiar with them through pictures or specimens in museums. See how every line in the flying-fish diagrams expresses speed in flying.

SAILBOATS

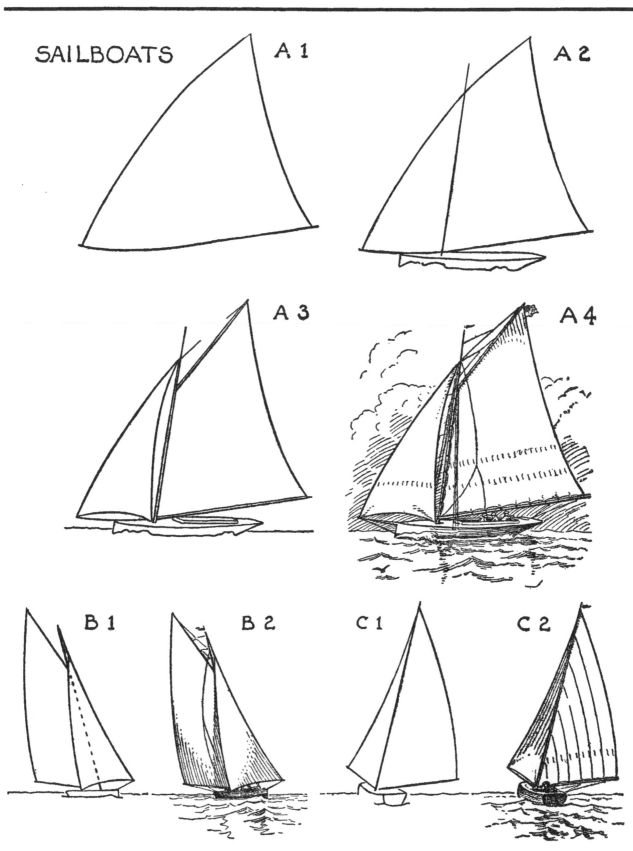

A 1

A 2

A 3

A 4

B 1

B 2

C 1

C 2

DOLLS

Here are some interesting subjects to draw. The first figure in each series—a circle for the head and a simple outline for the body and limbs—are to be sketched with careful thought with regard to the proportions. Notice that the eyes are placed in the lower half of the circle. To help you place them properly draw a line across the middle of the circle before you begin to draw the face.

After you have copied the dolls as they are pictured here, see how much imagination you have by clothing them in some other style of dress.

MORE DOLLS
TO DRAW

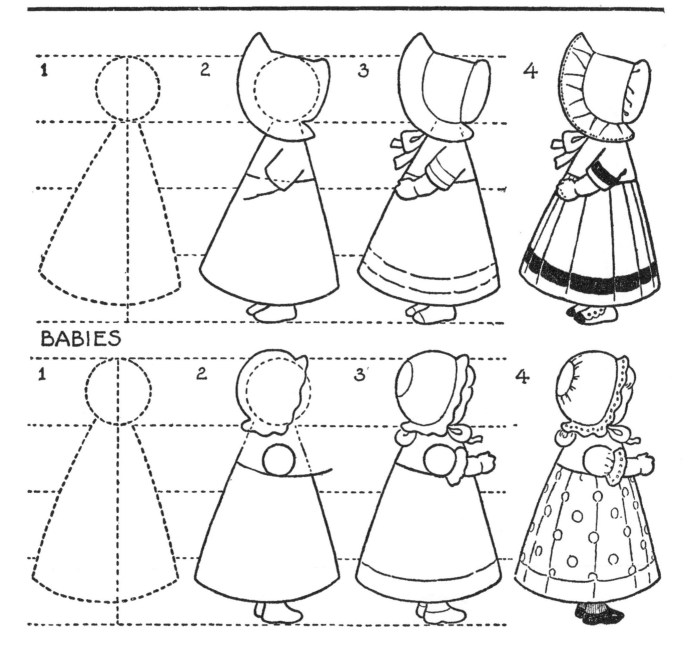

BABIES

When drawing the baby with the sunbonnet, or the one with the cap, begin by making a circle for the head and an apron-like form underneath it. Mark your first lines lightly and have the head one-fourth the entire height of the figure. Drawing the head of a figure just four times the height—as if dividing it —is called getting a figure in the proportion of four heads. This is the right proportion in which to draw pictures of very young children such as those on these two pages.

BABIES

You will notice in these engravings that parallel dotted lines are
indicated running across the diagrams. They are not intended
to be drawn by you just this way, but are only to remind you
of the right proportions in which to draw these pictures. Of
course, if it will help you in your work, you may mark them
when sketching. The children here are represented as standing before us very quietly. Farther on in the book you will be
given suggestions how to draw pictures of children in action.

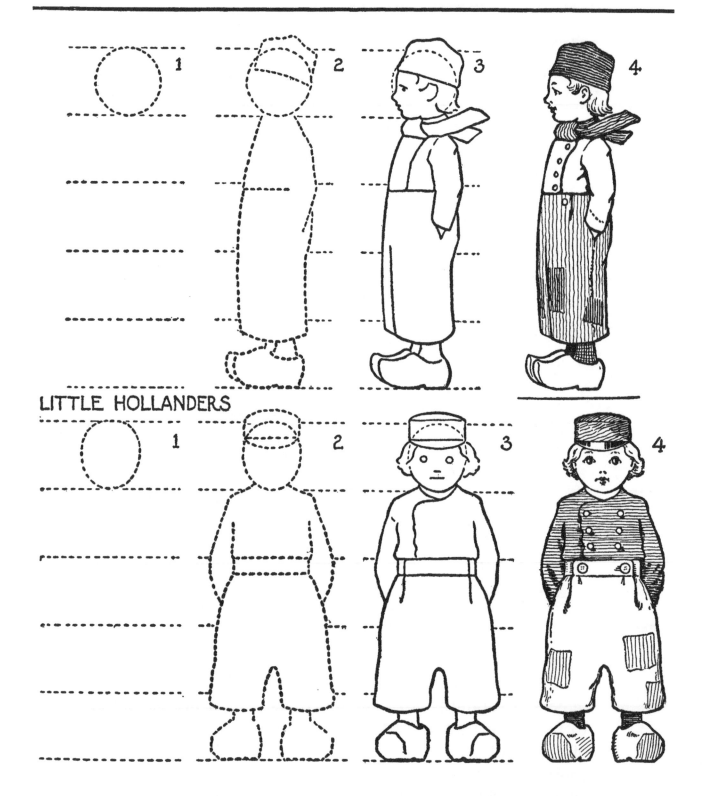

LITTLE HOLLANDERS

Here again parallel dotted lines cross the diagrams, to show you the proper proportions in which to draw these Little Hollanders. But on these pages the figures are drawn in five heads.

LITTLE HOLLANDERS

E.G.L.

The babies on preceding pages were drawn four heads high; the pictures on these pages are drawn five heads high because they represent older children.

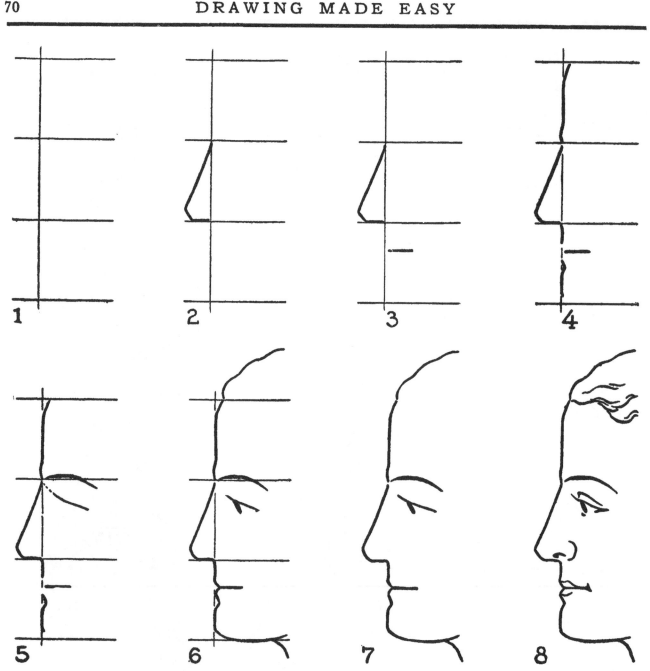

Drawing the side view of a face is shown above. In Figure 1, an up-and-down line is divided into three equal parts. As this is the foundation for the sketch, get it accurately marked. Notice that in Figure 3, the mouth comes at about one-third of that division.

On the opposite page are two lessons in drawing profile faces by simple, easy ways.

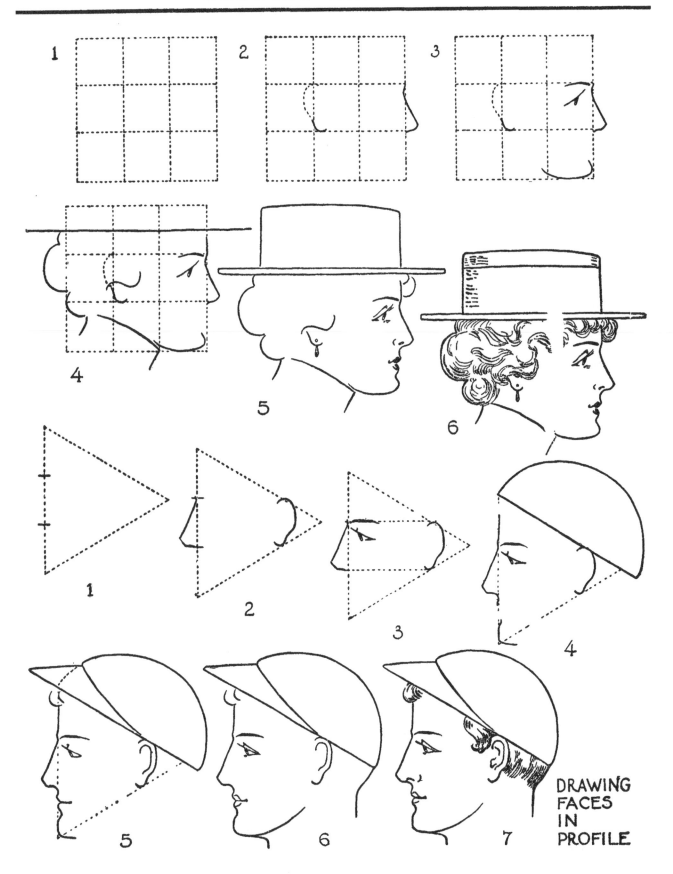

DRAWING
FACES
IN
PROFILE

BOYS' FACES

The first step that you take in starting out to draw one of the boys' faces is to make an oval-like form and draw the cross-lines through its centre. The line going across marks off the part of the head in which you place the lineaments, or lines that determine the drawing of the face. The up-and-down line helps in getting the lines evenly placed.

At the top of the opposite page is a face that will be easy to draw, as the way to go about making it is shown by the seven diagrams. The four faces with different expressions may be drawn in the same step-by-step process as that shown for the face with the placid countenance. The lower diagrams, A, B, C, and D, give the essential lines for the expressions depicted above them.

Compare the lines that make up the expression of the first face, the smiling one, with the lines of expression of the last one, the serious countenance. One set of lines are curved and pleasing, while the other set is characterized by angularity and severity.

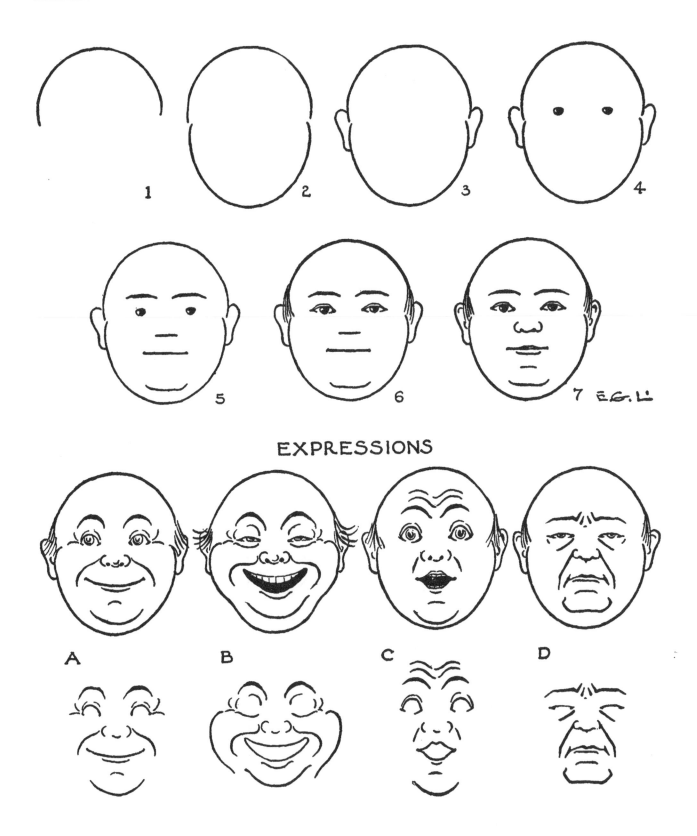

1   2   3   4

5   6   7 E.G.L.

EXPRESSIONS

A   B   C   D

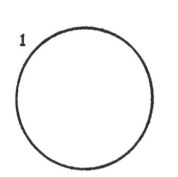

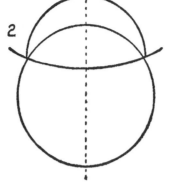

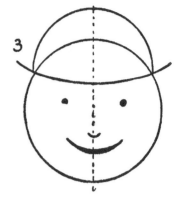

ROUND
FACE

E.G.L.

Whenever you feel in a playful mood and wish to make pictures
of droll-looking faces there is no harm at all in doing so.　Only
avoid making rude and ugly caricatures.

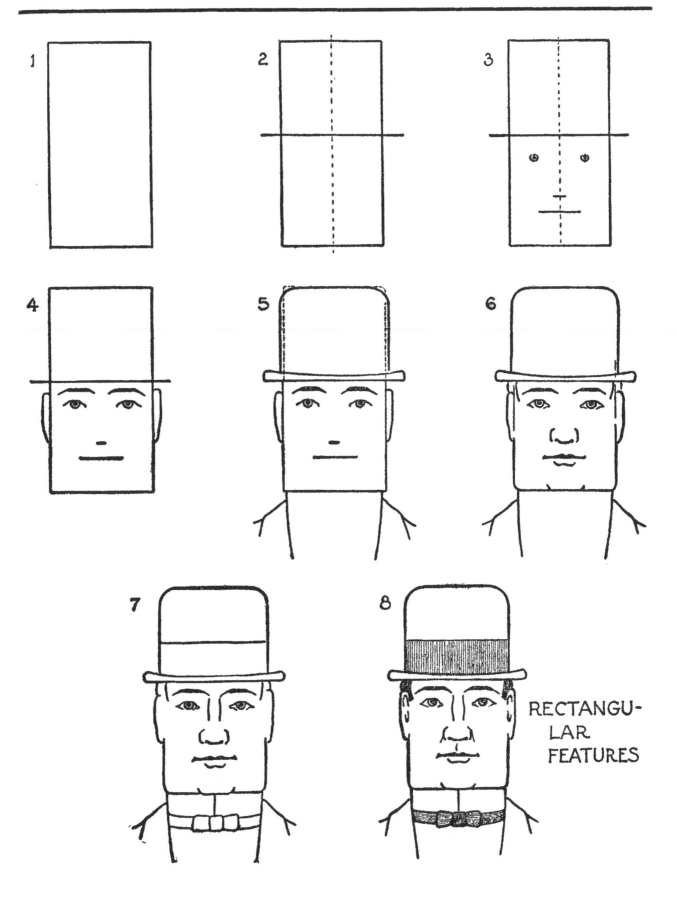

RECTANGU-
LAR
FEATURES

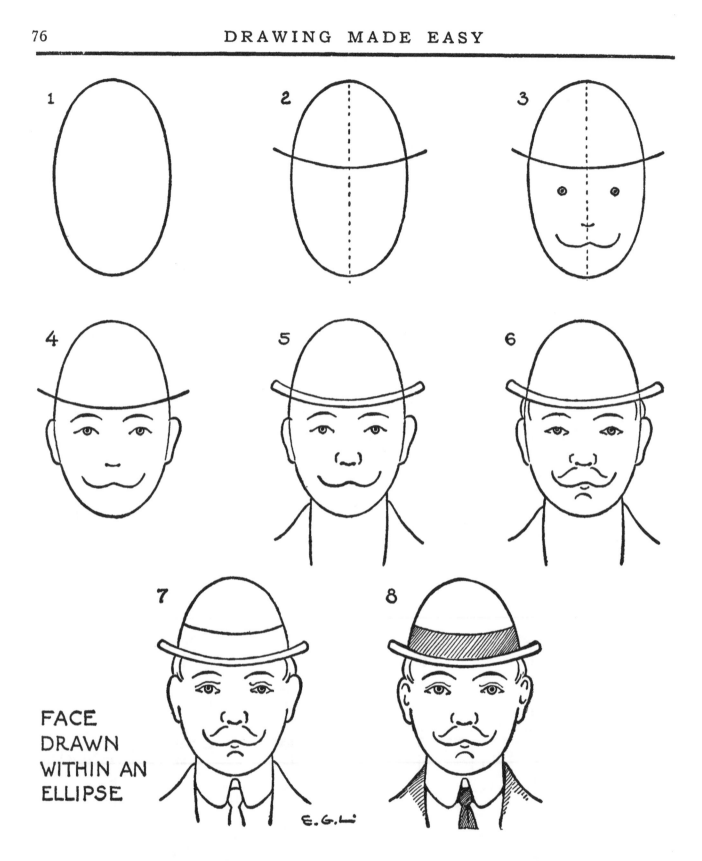

FACE
DRAWN
WITHIN AN
ELLIPSE

In these character sketches notice how the peculiarities of feature
of any particular face repeat themselves in that face.

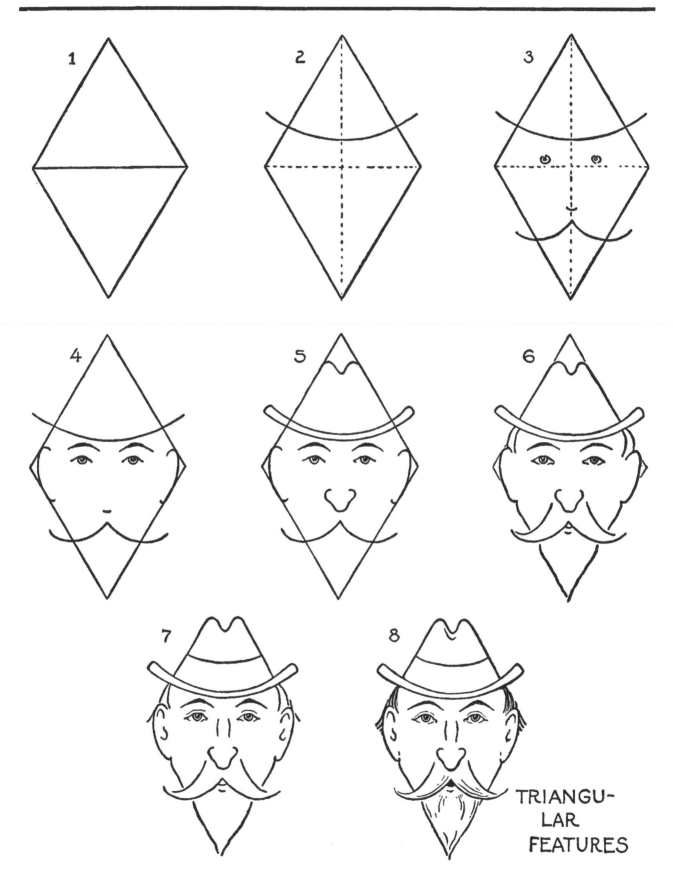

TRIANGU-
LAR
FEATURES

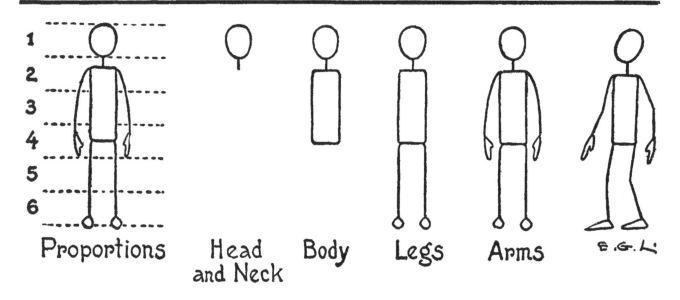

Proportions   Head   Body   Legs   Arms
                and Neck

SINGLE-LINE ACTION FIGURES

An oval-like outline for the head, a roughly drawn oblong for the
body, and four lines for the limbs are the few elements needed
to draw these figures. The limb lines can end in markings to
resemble hands and feet.

A few pages back babies were pictured in the proportion of four
heads, and some Little Hollanders in five heads. Now these
little action figures are planned to be six heads high. The
diagram at the top on the left shows this. Study this diagram
carefully, and, for the sake of practice, make many sketches of
the simple standing figure. When you have done this and
become familiar with the relative proportions of the figure,
study and draw the pictures showing them in action on the
following pages.

Note how balance is maintained by the bulk of the figure being
distributed equally on each side of a vertical line. But in
falling, you will see, a large part of the figure is on one side of
this vertical line. In a slow walk the figure seems nearly
balanced, but in running it is pictured as falling forward.

When you are uncertain as to which line to mark first in any of
these pictures, study the particular picture and find the line
that expresses the movement best. Keep that line in mind as
you draw.

Balance   Falling   Walking   Running

The slant of the body and the way the lines of the limbs are marked determine the degree of any action. But the placing on of the head, and getting its proper tilt, is just as important. This means thought before marking the direction of the short line representing the neck.

You can make many more sketches than those pictured here. Use this way of working for making pictures of the many activities of your play hours. Watch your companions at work and at play and see the attitudes that they take.

When you draw these little figures in action try to imagine yourself
   as going through the particular action that you are trying to
   sketch.   It helps wonderfully.
Study movement by the observation of the action of figures in the
   busy every-day world.

Make complete pictures of these little figures by clothing them.
Then you will see how much imagination you have.

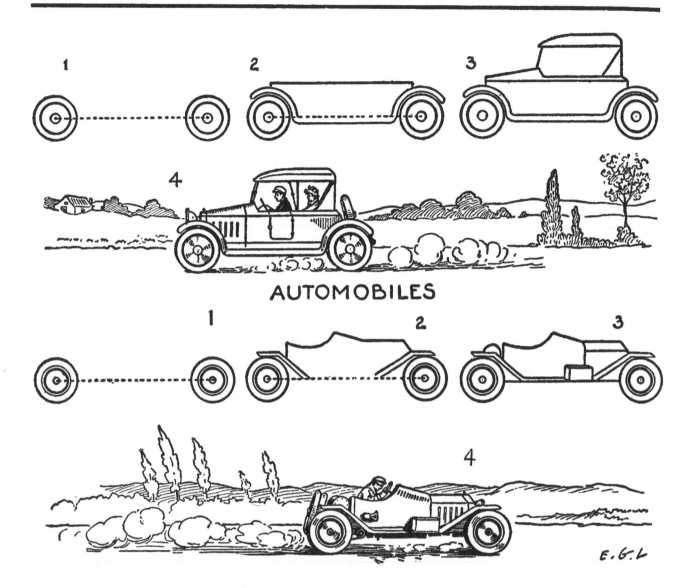

AUTOMOBILES

Two automobiles are pictured above the way they look when passing by on the road. The wheels in this case are circles; in sketching them, use the compasses, if you wish. If the automobiles were going in some other direction instead of passing directly before you, the wheels would present quite another appearance to your eye. They would take on the form of an ellipse and would need to be drawn free-hand.

When you draw the airplanes, notice the slant of the lines that define the wings. Certain groups of these lines go to an invisible point in the distance. The artist speaks of them as lines going off in perspective toward a vanishing point.

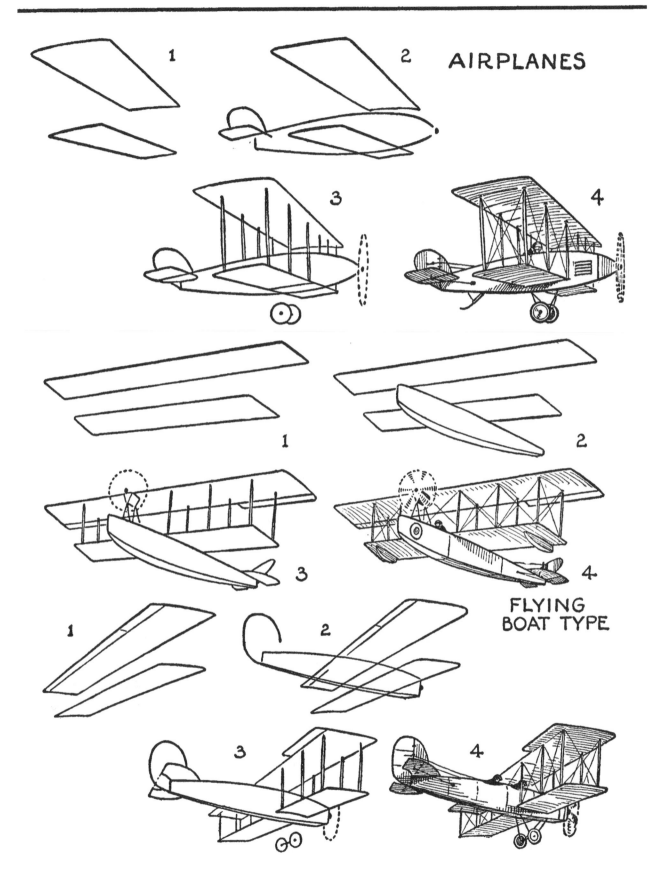

AIRPLANES

FLYING
BOAT TYPE

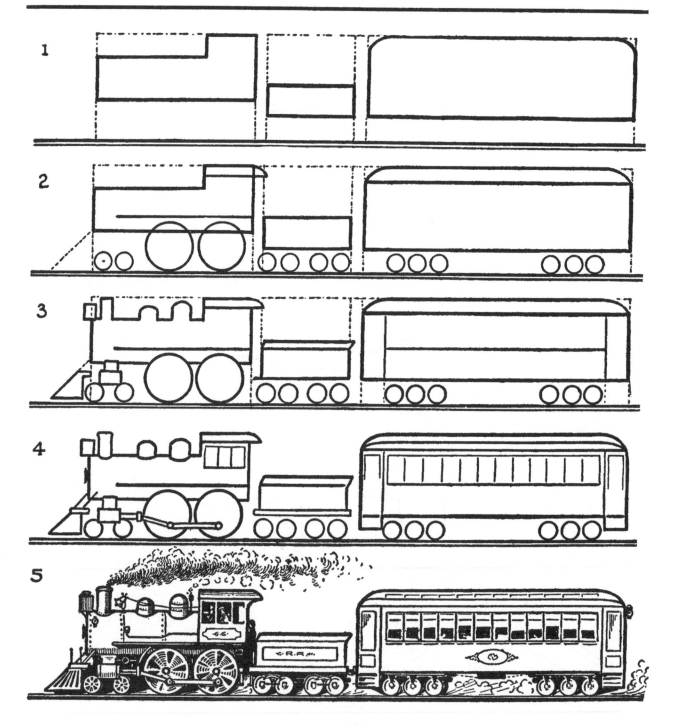

LOCOMOTIVE AND CAR

There is no objection, in copying the picture above, to a ruler for drawing the construction lines, nor of a triangle, to use with the ruler, in getting the right angles correctly.

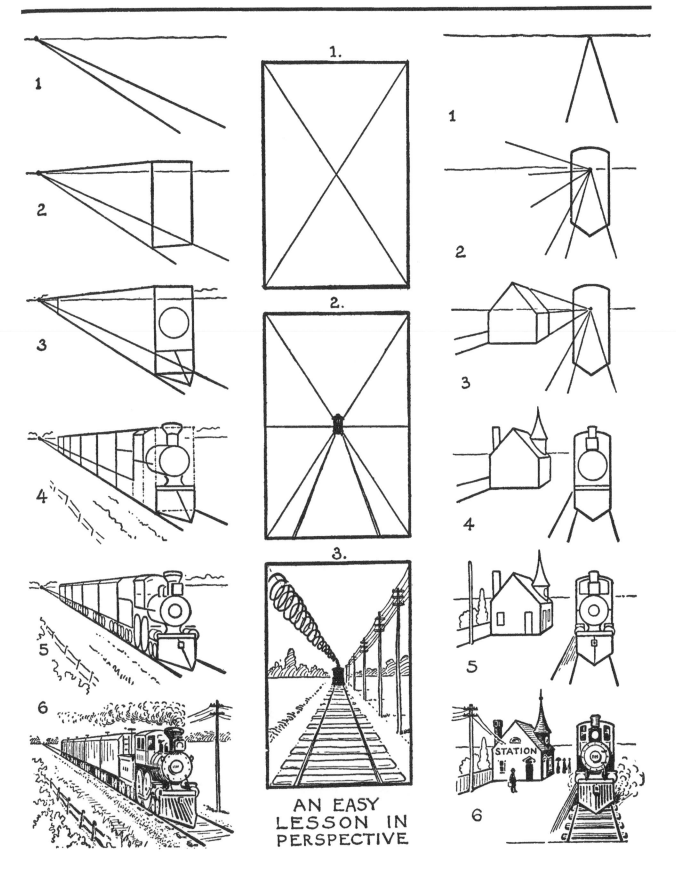

AN EASY
LESSON IN
PERSPECTIVE

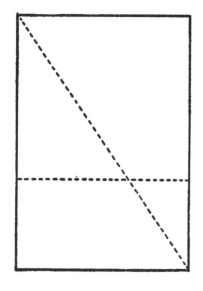

DRAWING LANDSCAPES

Here we have a few landscapes to study and draw. It is as important for you to study them as it is for you to make copies of them. There are altogether ten pictures, falling into three groups. Take the group on these two pages; note that they are all founded on the simple arrangement of lines shown by the diagram on this page. These lines serve three purposes: for one, they aid, if sketched in first, in drawing the various parts of the picture in their proper places; secondly, they link the parts of the picture together so that it has a sense of completeness; and, thirdly, they give the picture some interesting lines to attract and hold the attention of the eye.

The other groups of pictures, on the two following pages, have a little more complicated plan, or scheme of arrangement. But by marking a rectangle and then the leading lines, as shown, the picture-making goes on very rapidly.

Color your landscapes, if you wish, with the crayons, or water-color paints.

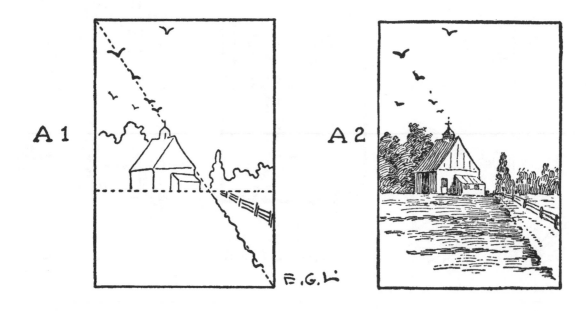

A 1

A 2

E.G.L.

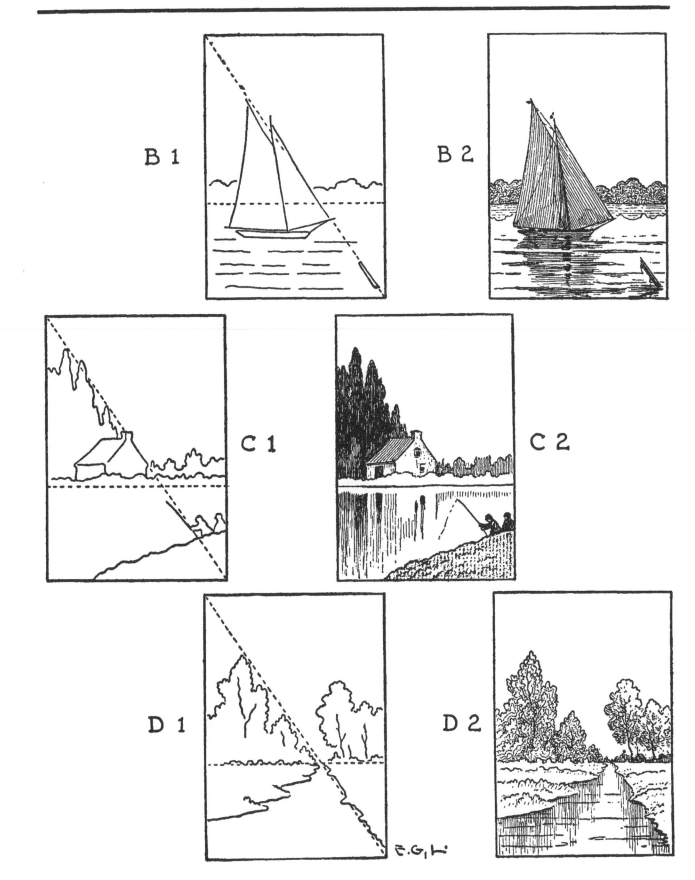

B 1

B 2

C 1

C 2

D 1

D 2

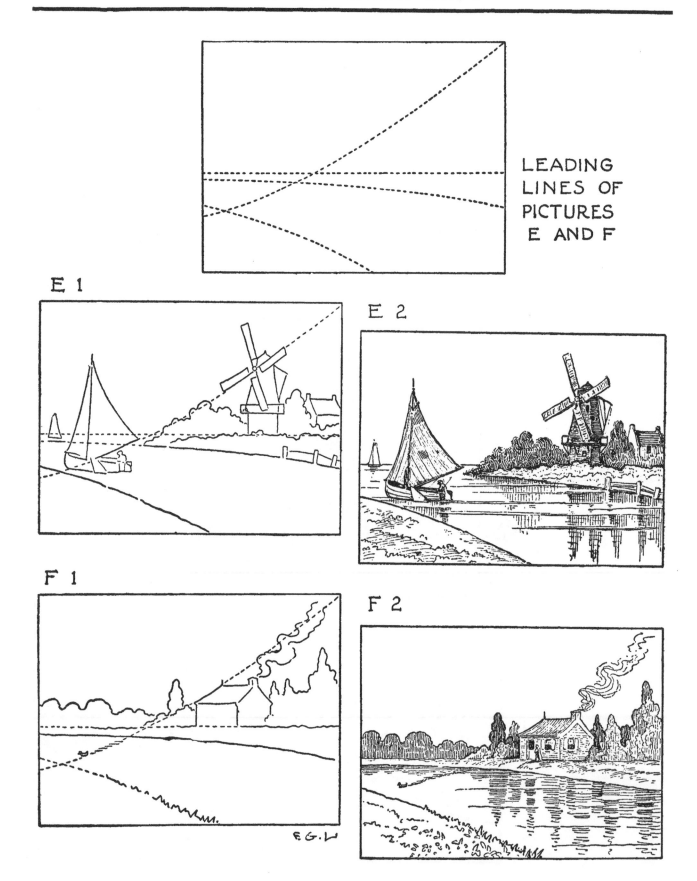

LEADING LINES OF PICTURES E AND F

E 1

E 2

F 1

F 2

LEADING LINES OF
PICTURES G, H, I AND J

G

H

I

J

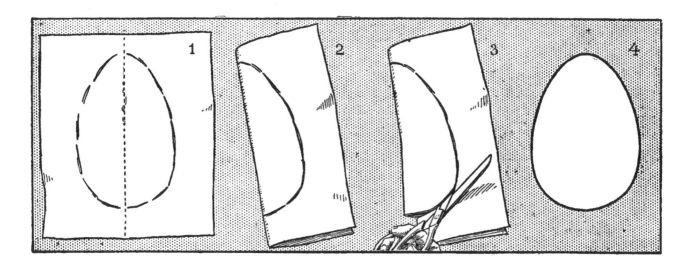

AN AID IN DRAWING OVALS

An oval has an outline like an egg, with one end rounder and fuller than the other. No doubt, when you have tried to draw an oval you have found it difficult to get it evenly shaped, with the outline firmly marked. One way in which you may draw an oval is to cut a pattern out first and then use this pattern by placing it against your sketching paper and tracing the outline by running the pencil around the edge.

The way to make an oval pattern for tracing is explained above.

1. Roughly sketch an oval on a sheet of paper.
2. Fold the paper so that the fold goes through the long middle line of the oval.
3. Cut out the oval, through the folded paper, with a pair of scissors. Cut with a firm, steady hand, so as to get it an even curve.
4. Open the paper, and you will have an oval pattern, with both sides even.

On the opposite page are a number of designs of shields, leaf designs, and ornaments which can be made in the same way as the oval. That is, first sketching out the intended design as accurately as possible, and then cutting it out when the paper has been folded.

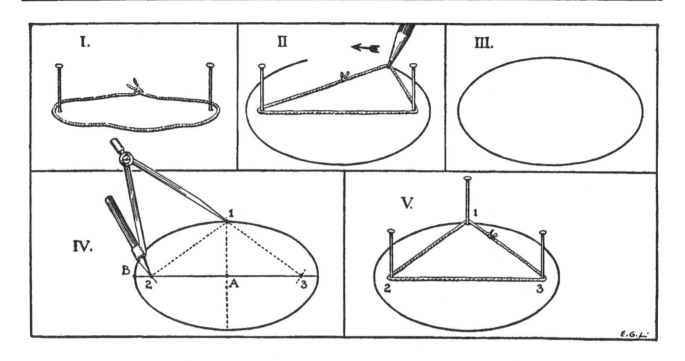

TO DRAW AN ELLIPSE

There is an important difference between an ellipse and an oval. In an oval the fulness of the two ends is not the same, while in an ellipse the two ends are exactly alike.

When you draw a wheel in any other position but one directly before you, give it the form of an ellipse. Turn back to the engraving on page 16, and see the comparison between a wheel in a side view and an ellipse.

Figures I and II of the engraving above show you how to go about drawing an ellipse.

To determine the places for the pins and the size of the loop:

    IV.   Take the pencil compasses and fix the legs so that they measure the distance from A to B. This is one-half of the long central line of the ellipse. Now place the point at 1, and have the pencil-point cross the long line at 2 and 3.

    V.   Stick pins into the paper at points 1, 2, and 3, and tie a string around them. Take out pin 1, and replace it with the point of the pencil, and then proceed with the problem as in Figure II.

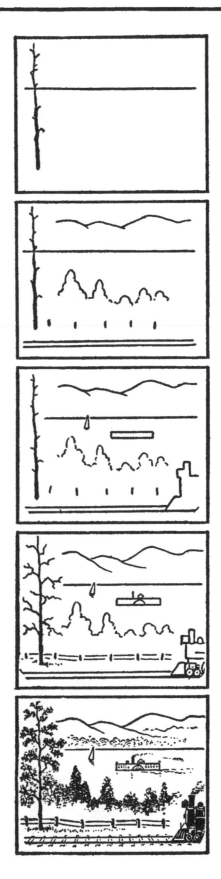